ABERDEEN

A HISTORY AND CELEBRATION
OF THE CITY

NORMAN M MILLER

THE FRANCIS FRITH COLLECTION

www.francisfrith.com

First published in the United Kingdom in 2005
by The Francis Frith Collection®

Hardback edition 2004 ISBN 1-84567-736-6
Paperback edition 2012 ISBN 978-1-84589-695-9

Text and Design copyright © The Francis Frith Collection®
Photographs copyright © The Francis Frith Collection®
except where indicated

The Frith® photographs and the Frith® logo are reproduced under
licence from Heritage Photographic Resources Ltd, the owners of the
Frith® archive and trademarks
'The Francis Frith Collection', 'Francis Frith' and 'Frith' are registered
trademarks of Heritage Photographic Resources Ltd.

British Library Cataloguing in Publication Data

Aberdeen - A History and Celebration of the City
Norman M Miller

The Francis Frith Collection®
Oakley Business Park, Wylye Road,
Dinton, Wiltshire SP3 5EU
Tel: +44 (0) 1722 716 376
Email: info@francisfrith.co.uk
www.francisfrith.com

Printed and bound in Great Britain
Contains material sourced from responsibly managed forests

Front Cover: **ABERDEEN, UNION STREET c1900** A90309t

Additional modern photographs by Norman M Miller.

Domesday extract used in timeline by kind permission of
Alecto Historical Editions, www.domesdaybook.org
Aerial photographs reproduced under licence from
Simmons Aerofilms Limited.
Historical Ordnance Survey maps reproduced under licence from
Homecheck.co.uk

Every attempt has been made to contact copyright holders of
illustrative material. We will be happy to give full acknowledgement in
future editions for any items not credited. Any information should be
directed to The Francis Frith Collection.

*The colour-tinting in this book is for illustrative purposes only,
and is not intended to be historically accurate*

AS WITH ANY HISTORICAL DATABASE, THE FRANCIS FRITH ARCHIVE IS
CONSTANTLY BEING CORRECTED AND IMPROVED, AND THE PUBLISHERS
WOULD WELCOME INFORMATION ON OMISSIONS OR INACCURACIES

Contents

ABERDEEN FROM THE AIR 1938 AF60052

Historical Timeline for Aberdeen

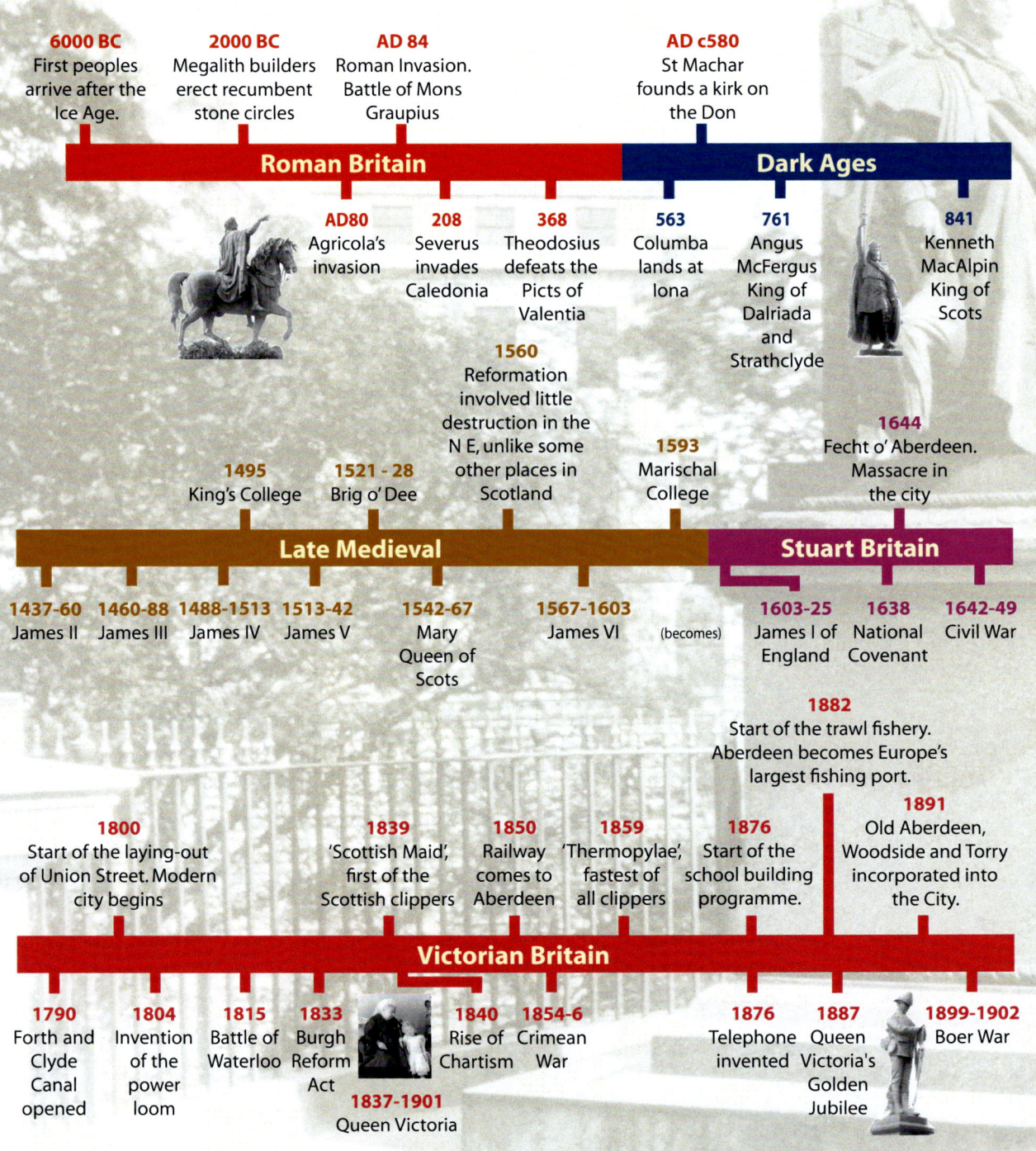

6000 BC
First peoples arrive after the Ice Age.

2000 BC
Megalith builders erect recumbent stone circles

AD 84
Roman Invasion. Battle of Mons Graupius

AD c580
St Machar founds a kirk on the Don

Roman Britain

Dark Ages

AD80
Agricola's invasion

208
Severus invades Caledonia

368
Theodosius defeats the Picts of Valentia

563
Columba lands at Iona

761
Angus McFergus King of Dalriada and Strathclyde

841
Kenneth MacAlpin King of Scots

1560
Reformation involved little destruction in the N E, unlike some other places in Scotland

1593
Marischal College

1644
Fecht o' Aberdeen. Massacre in the city

1495
King's College

1521 - 28
Brig o' Dee

Late Medieval

Stuart Britain

1437-60
James II

1460-88
James III

1488-1513
James IV

1513-42
James V

1542-67
Mary Queen of Scots

1567-1603
James VI

(becomes)

1603-25
James I of England

1638
National Covenant

1642-49
Civil War

1882
Start of the trawl fishery. Aberdeen becomes Europe's largest fishing port.

1891
Old Aberdeen, Woodside and Torry incorporated into the City.

1800
Start of the laying-out of Union Street. Modern city begins

1839
'Scottish Maid', first of the Scottish clippers

1850
Railway comes to Aberdeen

1859
'Thermopylae', fastest of all clippers

1876
Start of the school building programme.

Victorian Britain

1790
Forth and Clyde Canal opened

1804
Invention of the power loom

1815
Battle of Waterloo

1833
Burgh Reform Act

1840
Rise of Chartism

1854-6
Crimean War

1876
Telephone invented

1887
Queen Victoria's Golden Jubilee

1899-1902
Boer War

1837-1901
Queen Victoria

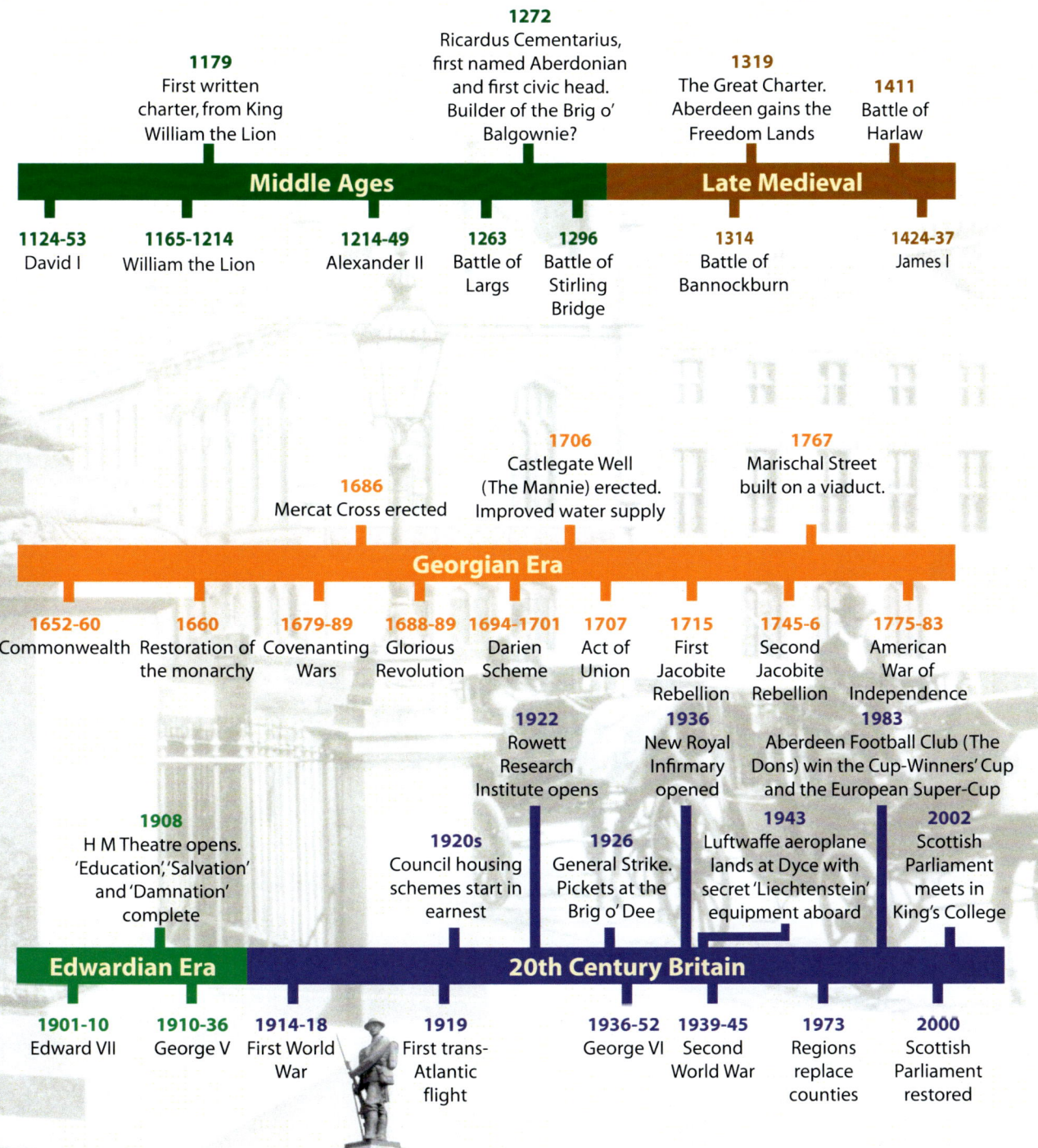

1179
First written charter, from King William the Lion

1272
Ricardus Cementarius, first named Aberdonian and first civic head. Builder of the Brig o' Balgownie?

1319
The Great Charter. Aberdeen gains the Freedom Lands

1411
Battle of Harlaw

Middle Ages

Late Medieval

1124-53
David I

1165-1214
William the Lion

1214-49
Alexander II

1263
Battle of Largs

1296
Battle of Stirling Bridge

1314
Battle of Bannockburn

1424-37
James I

1686
Mercat Cross erected

1706
Castlegate Well (The Mannie) erected. Improved water supply

1767
Marischal Street built on a viaduct.

Georgian Era

1652-60
Commonwealth

1660
Restoration of the monarchy

1679-89
Covenanting Wars

1688-89
Glorious Revolution

1694-1701
Darien Scheme

1707
Act of Union

1715
First Jacobite Rebellion

1745-6
Second Jacobite Rebellion

1775-83
American War of Independence

1922
Rowett Research Institute opens

1936
New Royal Infirmary opened

1983
Aberdeen Football Club (The Dons) win the Cup-Winners' Cup and the European Super-Cup

1908
H M Theatre opens. 'Education', 'Salvation' and 'Damnation' complete

1920s
Council housing schemes start in earnest

1926
General Strike. Pickets at the Brig o' Dee

1943
Luftwaffe aeroplane lands at Dyce with secret 'Liechtenstein' equipment aboard

2002
Scottish Parliament meets in King's College

Edwardian Era

20th Century Britain

1901-10
Edward VII

1910-36
George V

1914-18
First World War

1919
First trans-Atlantic flight

1936-52
George VI

1939-45
Second World War

1973
Regions replace counties

2000
Scottish Parliament restored

CHAPTER ONE

Two Towns Emerge from the Mists of Time

THE RIVERS DEE AND DON flow into the North Sea within three miles of each other, just north of where the Grampian mountains extend to the coast, pushing the main routes from north to south far over to the east. In this pivotal position, the royal burgh of Aberdeen grew where the routes from north, south and west came together, plus, of course, the sea route from the east.

Just before the Dee reaches the sea, its waters spread out into shallow mud flats, covered at high tide, but partly exposed as the tide ebbed. This place was known as the Inches, from the Celtic word for islands. In this natural harbour vessels could lie in safety, protected from storms by the long spit of sand that separates the Inches from the open sea. Rising steeply from the northern edge of the Inches was what was to become known as Castlehill. Here, the earliest inhabitants could see any danger approaching and build some sort of protective structure for themselves.

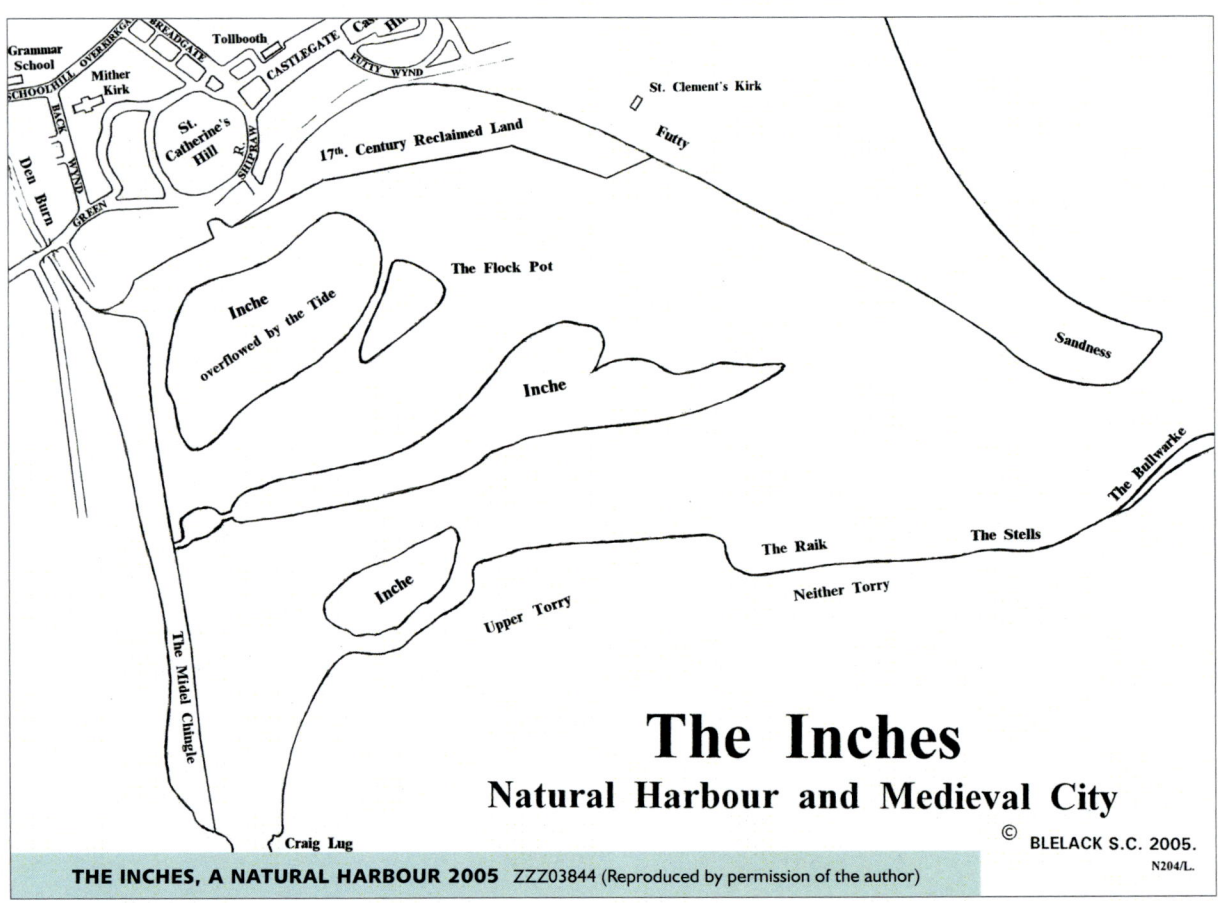

THE INCHES, A NATURAL HARBOUR 2005 ZZZ03844 (Reproduced by permission of the author)

Reclamation started in the early 17th century, as shown on Parson Gordon's beautiful city portrait of 1661. The small medieval city clusters around the Castlegate.

Long before any settled community was established, humans came to live in the area, following the retreat of the glaciers at the end of the last ice age. Some of them we know as Strand Loopers. They have left us shell middens; large piles of shells from the shellfish that formed an important part of their diet. Much later, about four millennia ago, people all over the British Isles were erecting stone circles. Huge stones, sometimes weighing several tons, were dragged to the tops of hills. This effort was stupendous, especially as the builders did not have any mechanical devices to help with the work. In the north-east, as an indication of things to come, we went our own way. A large stone was laid on its side, with the two tallest uprights at either end. In many parts of the rural north-east, these unique recumbent stone circles can still be seen. Ancient structures do not often survive urbanisation. But within the city boundary, at the edge of a high plateau, is the Lang Stene at Hilton, a huge monolith, perhaps the sole survivor of a circle. The built-up area surrounded it in the 1920s.

THE CITY'S ARMORIAL BEARINGS 2005 A90719k (Norman Miller)

Here carved in granite on the Victorian Town House, these indicate the age and status of the city. Only Perth and Aberdeen have the Royal Tressure of Scotland on their arms.

Later still, about two millennia ago, the Roman legions marched across Caledonia. Did men from what was to become Aberdeen join the combined force of the Celtic peoples who fought in AD 84 at the battle of Mons Graupius, the earliest recorded battle in the north-east? The Romans won the battle, but decided not to attempt a permanent subjugation of our land. So while places to the south have the foundations of villas and inscribed gravestones to show that the Romans had been there, we have only the spectral outlines of marching camps, and a few Roman fish-hooks found in the estuary of the Dee. Perhaps the men of the Roman navy, who followed the legions as they moved north, enjoyed some Dee salmon. It is from the account of this Roman expedition, written by Tacitus, son-in-law of Agricola, the commander of the invaders, that we derive the name 'Grampian'. A medieval scribe wrote down an 'm' instead of the original 'u' in 'Graupius'. Thus is derived the name of Britain's highest mountain range.

The earliest official reference to the existence of Aberdeen as a community comes with the royal charter granted to the burgh in 1179 by William the Lion, King of Scots. In this charter, as in many others of similar date, the king states that he is confirming the charter granted by David I, his grandfather. No charter of King David's time exists anywhere in Scotland. It may be that, previous to William the Lion's time, the king only spoke in the presence of witnesses when granting charters. This tiny charter is the oldest of a huge collection of historic

The Name of the City

The name 'Aberdeen' is a mystery. 'Aber' is a Brythonic (Welsh-like Celtic) prefix, meaning 'near the mouth of'. 'Aber' names are common in Wales, but in Scotland there are also 'Inver' names. This is the Gaelic (Celtic of Ireland and western Scotland) equivalent and these names are later, dating from the time of Irish missionaries from Iona, from the 6th century onwards. Usually, what comes after the prefix is the name of the river. But 'deen' is neither Dee nor Don. It could be either or both! The 'Aber' prefix suggests that the name is very old. Has there been a settled community here since Roman times or earlier?

documents carefully preserved by the city council over a period of more than eight centuries. This splendid archive is the most complete set of civic records in Scotland and probably in Britain, apart from those of London. They are stored securely in the Town House, Aberdeen's municipal headquarters in the middle of the city.

During the following two centuries, English armies marched all over Scotland as the English kings tried to establish suzerainty over the whole of the British Isles. According to one contemporary historical account, one hundred English ships were burnt in Aberdeen harbour by rebels supporting William Wallace. There probably was some fire under this smoke, but, as was often the case, numbers were greatly exaggerated. It is unlikely that the English had so many vessels to bring north. However the city's support for the Bruce in the following years shows that this was not just idle boasting. When King

Robert the Bruce was leading the fight for Scottish sovereignty against the English, the citizens of Aberdeen were his consistent and determined supporters. It is said that he was hidden in one of the burgh's friaries when he was too ill to travel. The citizens combined one night to attack the English garrison, which was building a castle on the Castlehill. The attack was a success. The garrison were all killed, and the castle was dismantled to prevent its use by any future English expedition. It is suggested that the city's motto, 'Bon Accord' (the good agreement), was first used as the password for those who assembled to make this attack. But the great historian of Bruce's times, John Barbour, himself an Aberdonian, does not mention it. This simply makes the story all the more remarkable. What is certain is that, for many centuries, this motto has been used with great pride by Aberdonians and remains part of the city's coat of arms to this day.

MUNICIPAL BUILDINGS 1892 A90301

This is where Aberdeen was to go. It would take seven centuries from the granting of the first written royal charter. The dark spire in the foreground is that of the Tollbooth, the old headquarters of the council, built about 1616. The Town House extends from there to the taller tower, built about 1870. The statue is of George, fifth and last Duke of Gordon, as the inscription on the plinth poignantly explains. This is one of the first, if not the first, statue to be carved in granite for over a thousand years.

THE WILLIAM WALLACE STATUE 1935 SA000017
(Courtesy of University of St Andrews Library)

Did you know?

Many Aberdonians think that William Wallace's left arm was sent to Aberdeen after his execution, to be displayed as a warning to others who might think of rebelling. However, it was not! So great was Wallace's prestige as a tragic hero that people wanted to do something for him, even if it was only after his death. The story is that Scottish patriots gave his arm a decent burial in the kirkyard of Nigg, just south of the Dee.

Following the decisive Scottish victory in 1314 at Bannockburn, Robert the Bruce was able to reward those who had been his friends in the long conflict. He granted the Great Charter to the city. Since 1179, several charters had been issued. Bruce's charter of 1319 was different, for he granted to the city the land on which it stood, the foreshore between the rivers and the royal forest of the Stocket.

The magistrates of Aberdeen were now collectively the feudal lord, with the right to rent out their land. The grant did not come entirely free, although the land has ever since been called the Freedom Lands. A feu duty of £213 6s 8d was payable to the king every year. But, once agreed, a feu duty never changes, while as decades and centuries proceed, the rents charged by the local superior rise. The city of Aberdeen had gained a substantial income.

Two miles to the north of Aberdeen was Old Aberdeen. It is likely that Old Aberdeen is not as old as Aberdeen. Perhaps the royal burgh, with its greater size and wealth and its international contacts, was more modern than its smaller neighbour. That name, Old Aberdeen, is certainly appropriate now, as the burgh contains many beautiful Victorian, Georgian and even older buildings.

Like Rome, Old Aberdeen has a creation myth. St Machar, a companion on Iona of St Columba, was inspired to look for a place where a river bent in the shape of a shepherd's crook, an important symbol for early Christians. This he found on the Don, not far from the sea. Did the holy man build a house for himself and a place for his new converts to worship atop the steep bank that overlooks the crook? Certainly the cathedral of St Machar stands there today.

The two towns were not united into a single political entity until 1891.

In a city lying between two rivers, bridges are more than usually important. There is some evidence of there having been a bridge over the Dee at the foot of the old road from the south, the Causeway Mounth, about two miles west of Aberdeen. This would have been a wooden structure, which tend not to survive. The two rivers are very different from one another, as expressed in the old rhyme:

'Ae mile o' Don's worth twa o' Dee,
Except for salmon, fish and tree.'

The Don wanders through rolling country, good for agriculture. The steep, rugged valley of the Dee has the best scenery. But this all changes as the rivers approach the sea. Here it is the Dee that has gentle banks, while the Don passes through steep slopes clad with mature trees and then flows through a gorge with almost vertical sides just half a mile from its mouth.

It is here at the issue of the gorge that the Brig o' Balgownie dramatically strides over the Don at the one place on the lower reaches of either river where a single arch could be thrown across. It is believed that the Brig was constructed by Ricardus Cementarius (Richard the Builder), the first Aberdonian whose name has come down to us, and the first recorded civic head of our city. If so, the Brig must date from the 1290s, as we know that Richard died then. It was certainly in existence in 1320, when King Robert the Bruce granted money to the city to repair it. For four centuries it was to be the only bridge on the whole length of the Don.

The only remaining building in the royal burgh that dates from this time is St Nicholas, the Mither Kirk of Aberdeen. But only a small part of the existing structure is so old. Kirks are frequently rebuilt as their communities become more prosperous and, as the parish kirk of a royal burgh, St Nicholas was more prosperous than most. The north transept, known as Collison's Aisle, dates from the 12th or even from the 11th century. It has recently been made into a chapel for the oil industry and a memorial to those who have died working in it. It is dedicated to St John the Evangelist, patron saint of oil workers. The oldest bit of the oldest building in the city has the most modern of functions.

ST MACHAR'S CATHEDRAL c1900 A90321

A late 15th-century rebuilding of earlier work, this may be Europe's only medieval cathedral built of granite. Today, it is the parish kirk of Old Aberdeen. This view has hardly changed in the century since the photograph was taken.

THE BRIG O' BALGOWNIE c1890 A90304

Already six centuries old when this was taken, the scale of the engineering is obvious. The beauty of the situation can scarcely be exaggerated. It is an excellent combination of the drama of nature and artifice reinforcing one another. The building to the left is Nether Don, originally a salmon fishing station, now a private house. Many of the houses in the background have recently been modernised after some of them had lain empty for years. The foreground is now covered in mature trees.

CORONATION CELEBRATIONS 1953 ZZZ03851
(Author's Collection)

Always aware of its status as a royal burgh, Aberdeen was determined to celebrate the coronation of Queen Elizabeth II in style. As well as concerts, sports displays and fireworks, there was a historical pageant of seven episodes from the city's past.

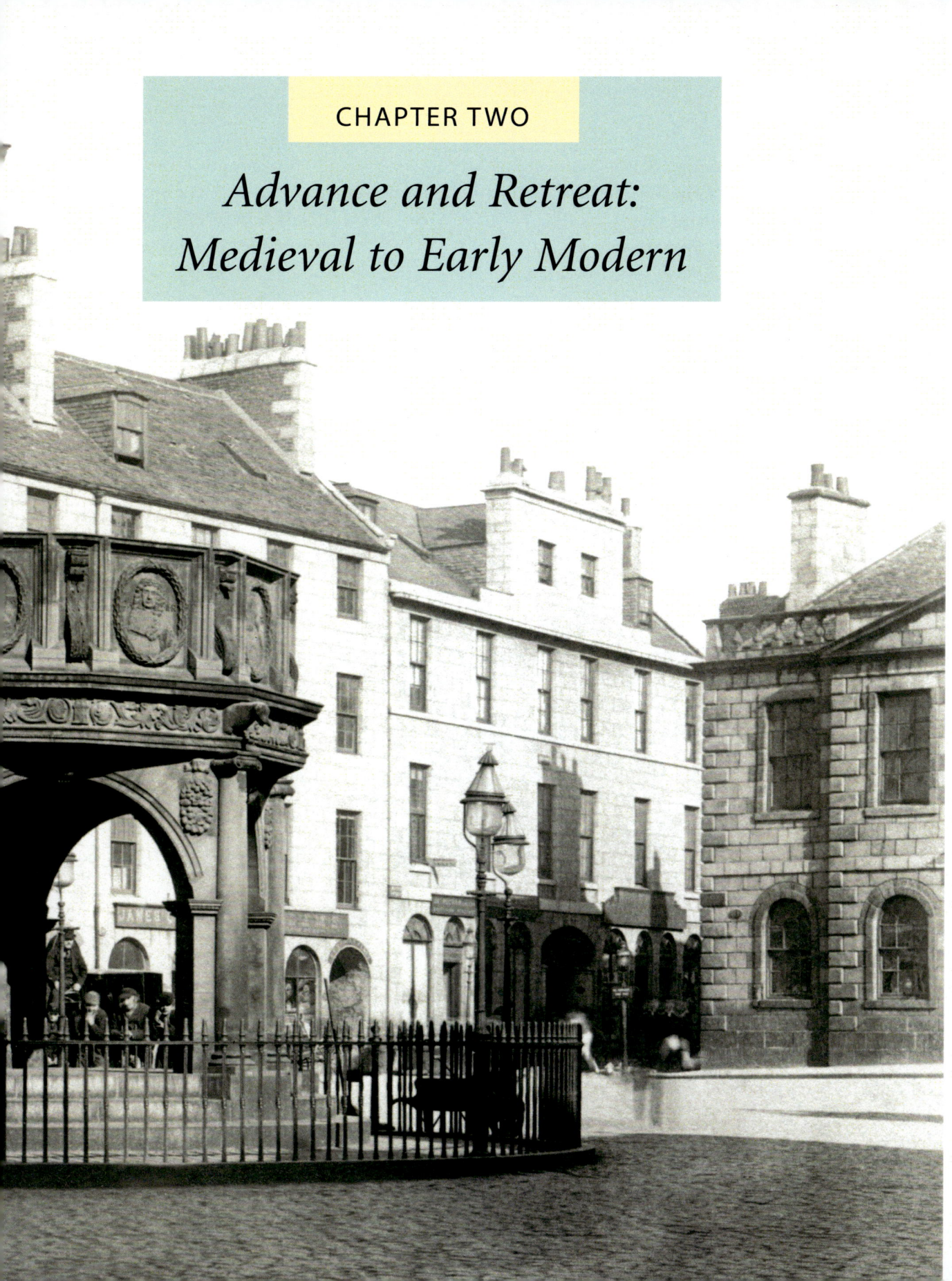

CHAPTER TWO

Advance and Retreat: Medieval to Early Modern

THE CITY had enjoyed its new prosperity for less than a century, when, in 1411, the north-east felt itself threatened by the advance of an army of Highlanders, led by Donald MacDonald, the Lord of the Isles, who was intent on claiming the earldom of Buchan for himself. The lowland lairds (country landlords) combined to resist this challenge and prominent among them was the city's provost. (A provost is the name given to the chief civic officer of a Scottish town). The two armies met about twenty miles north of the city, Provost Davidson leading a small band of citizens into battle. The engagement was indecisive, but the Highlanders withdrew and never again seriously threatened the security of the lowland elite.

The battle of Harlaw in 1411 became a major aspect of the city's belief about itself, perhaps mainly because the provost,

THE ALBERT MEMORIAL c1870 SA000007 (Courtesy of University of St Andrews Library)

The statue of Prince Albert had been unveiled by Queen Victoria in one of her first public appearances in widowhood. In the background is the New Trinity Hall, designed in 1846 by John Smith and his son, William. This earned John Smith the nickname Tudor Johnnie. It was the headquarters of the Incorporated Trades after they moved from the former property of the Trinity Friars. More powerful than the trades were the merchants, the burgesses of guild, who came to have the exclusive right to be town councillors and thus to control the local laws.

Sir Robert Davidson, was among those who died there. (His knighthood may have been a posthumous courtesy title.) Successive generations were intensely proud of their ancestors' part in the battle. On the 500th anniversary, in 1911, the council decided to build a memorial to the event. It is one of the largest battlefield memorials in Britain. When playing fields were laid out for the public schools (in Scotland public schools belong to and are open for the whole of the public), these were called the Harlaw Fields. Despite the occasional emergency, Aberdeen gradually became more prosperous.

Guilds, know as the seven Incorporated Trades, controlled the skilled work done in the city. The trades were the bakers, fleshers, hammermen, shoemakers, tailors, weavers and wrights and coopers. Hammermen were metal workers. They included blacksmiths and jewellers and, somewhere in between, silversmiths. Aberdeen Art Gallery has several beautiful items of their 18th- and 19th-century work. The trades still exist, although now largely as a social grouping. In 1966 they moved into new premises, whose faceless concrete ugliness is made tolerable only by being set back from the streets. They reinstalled in the new building the stained glass windows taken from their old building.

In medieval times Aberdeen was to become Scotland's greatest port. Exports were mostly raw materials, like grain and timber, while imports included luxuries, such as fine cloth, tableware and wine. One luxury item that was exported was salmon. The city had rights over the salmon fishery in the Dee and Don estuaries. This was sometimes worth as much as the land to the local exchequer.

The city was the only coastal royal burgh in the county of Aberdeen. This meant that it had a monopoly of foreign trade for the whole county, a factor which greatly increased the wealth of the city and especially of the merchant burgesses, who had a monopoly of this trade. One beneficiary of this prosperity was the Kirk of St Nicholas, which, maintained by the municipal authorities, grew to be the largest parish kirk in Scotland.

When the kirk that St Machar had founded was made a cathedral in the 13th century, it boosted the importance and the size of Old Aberdeen. There was a bishop as well as a dean and chapter and various officials needed to run the complex organisation of a diocese. The road from the cathedral to the main road through the little town was lined with the large houses they occupied. It is still called Chanonry, the collective noun for canons, the senior priests of the diocese.

Another source of Old Aberdeen's prosperity was that very main road, along which the trade to and from the royal burgh had to pass. Here was a convenient place to hold markets for local goods, as well as two annual fairs, attracting vendors and customers from a much wider background. The proximity of the larger town brought many opportunities. In Old Aberdeen too there were guilds organising the work of local craftsmen. Indeed there is still a very small street that rejoices in the name Wrights' and Coopers' Place.

WRIGHTS' AND COOPERS' PLACE 2005 A90722k (Norman Miller)

A quiet corner in Old Aberdeen.

In 1495, something really dramatic happened. Bishop Elphinstone set up a university. There were few staff and only some dozens of students, but it increased both the prosperity and the prestige of the town. The buildings were named King's College, in honour of the direct interest that King James IV took in the new university. From the start, encouraged by its royal patron, the university taught medicine, the first to do so in Britain.

Did you know?

From 1495, Scotland had three universities, while England had only two. By 1598, Scotland had five universities, while England still had only two. From 1593 to 1860, until they were united, Aberdeen had two universities, the same number as the whole of England had till 1830! But since 1992, when Robert Gordon's Institute of Technology was given university status, Aberdeen again has two universities. (England has gained a few more since 1830.)

KING'S COLLEGE c1900 A90322

The Crown Tower and the chapel, which can just be seen beyond it, date from 1500. This chapel contains the best-preserved ecclesiastical woodwork in Scotland. The crown is that of the Holy Roman Emperor, symbolising the universality of the education to be provided. The buildings in the foreground were erected in 1830; built in the same freestone from Spynie, in Moray. The railings have long since been removed.

There had been plans for a bridge over the River Dee for quite a long time, but they were never implemented until 1521. The bridging site chosen was a shallow place, close to the end of the main road from the south and more than two miles west of the city. A bridge of seven round arches was built here, the arches all being of the same profile. There was no need for it to be as high as the Brig o' Balgownie, as the banks on both sides were fairly low. But, as at Balgownie, one bank, that on the south in this instance, was higher than the other. So here too there had to be a raised causeway to gain access to the bridge.

While the Brig o' Balgownie had been built in local and mixed materials, the Brig o' Dee was constructed of freestone, imported from Moray. The use of a uniform building material gives a unity to the whole structure. In the days when there were only a handful of bridges in the whole of Scotland and only one other in the north-east, this long structure must have inspired awe. It was built very narrow and would have looked to a traveller crossing it even longer than it does today. But, in case there should be more traffic than expected, the cutwaters are all carried up to parapet level, where they support refuges, some of which are even provided with seats.

Not content with a merely functional structure, the bridge was decorated with the armorial bearings of the men of importance. Over time, several were added. Sadly, they have all been neglected for a long time and many are close to being completely defaced.

The bridge was widened by about half of its original width in 1840. It continues to be used by vehicles to-day, although the heaviest of these are now directed to the 20th-century bridge half a mile downstream. The refuges are now really useful as the carriageway is just wide enough for two motor-cars to pass and the pavement is very narrow. So if pedestrians are going in different directions across the bridge, it is necessary for one to wait there for the other to pass.

In 1560, Scotland went Protestant, by Act of Parliament. By the standards of the day, the Reformation here was a civilised and tolerant affair, with little real persecution by either side. This was nowhere more true than in the north-east, where a kind of ecumenism occurred. The Protestant Lords, led by the Earl Marischal, seized much

THE BRIDGE OF DEE c1900 A90310

The bridge was built to designs by Alexander Galloway, Rector of Kinkell, started in 1521 and widened by John Smith, 1840. The upstream facings were removed and replaced on the widened structure. The only visible evidence of the widening is the use of granite in the piers. This view has changed little, although there would now be houses and supermarkets just out of the picture.

of the Kirk's wealth and the Catholics, lead by the Earl of Huntly, took the rest. John Knox, leader of the Reformation in Scotland, wanted to establish a school in every parish. No wonder, then, that he did not achieve this. Even so, the high regard for education that inspired the reformers left its mark. Scotland was to become one of the best-educated nations before compulsory schooling was introduced.

Not long before the Reformation, St Machar's Cathedral had been decorated with a heraldic ceiling along the nave. At one side, the armorial bearings of the King of Scots are followed by those of the great lords of the realm. On the other side, there are those of the Holy Roman Emperor, followed by the chief monarchs of Europe. Henry VIII of England comes fourth. In the middle come the bishops of Scotland, with the Pope at their head. In many places, so popish a display would have been removed and burnt. Here, they survive. Not only did they survive the zeal of the reformers, they then survived the collapse of the central tower of the cathedral in the 1680s. Fortunately, it fell eastwards, leaving this beautiful ceiling to be appreciated and enjoyed today. A recent minister at St Machar's liked to say that he was the only minister in the Kirk who worked under the Pope.

One positive thing came out of the dubious practices of this period. The Earl Marischal granted some of his new property to found another university. Known as Marischal College, this was intended to be a truly Protestant college, while King's was believed

MARISCHAL COLLEGE 1878 SA000002
(Courtesy of University of St Andrews Library)

Unlike the older King's College, the original buildings do not survive. In the background here are the 1837 buildings by Archibald Simpson. Only the lower half of the tower dates from then. In the foreground are the late Victorian extensions. The obelisk in the quadrangle is in honour of Sir James MacGrigor (1771-1858), who, as a student, helped to start the Medico-Chirurgical Society and went on to start the Army Medical Corps.

to be secretly sympathetic to the old ways. The property the earl gave had belonged to the Greyfriars, one of four orders established in the city, all of them being disbanded at the Reformation. It stands on what is now called Broad Street, a medieval street in the city centre. A Presbyterian kirk, called Greyfriars, existed on the site until early in 2005.

To make sure that there was as little damage as possible at this time, the magistrates removed all the popish artifacts from the Mither Kirk of Aberdeen before the reformers arrived. The articles were then sold and the money raised used to fund improvements to the harbour. This was very appropriate, as a portion of the dues from the harbour had long been used to build up these same artifacts.

Did you know?

At the south end of the Brig o' Dee was a wayside chapel where people could pray before going on a journey. In the chapel was Our Lady of Aberdeen, a wooden statue of the Virgin Mary. During the Reformation, the statue, regarded as an idol, was thrown in the river. She floated out to sea, where she was found by Catholic Flemish fishermen who took her home to Flanders, where she still remains. Four centuries later, the Catholics established a new church in the south of the city and called it Our Lady of Aberdeen!

ABERDEEN GRAMMAR SCHOOL 2005 A90701k (Norman Miller)

Lord Byron looks on at the front of the 1863 Grammar School building. The keystone of the main doorway carries the initials AA P - Alexander Anderson. Provost.

The Grammar School

Older than the universities by perhaps a couple of centuries is Aberdeen Grammar School. Its reputation for first-class education continues to this day. The best-known former pupil is Lord Byron and the school is very proud of its connection with him. The most distinguished is James Gibbs, recognised as one of Britain's greatest architects. He designed St Martin-in-the-Fields, the church now overlooking Trafalgar Square in London. Sir Alexander Anderson, Aberdeen's foremost civic leader, was also a pupil here.

The Reformation was reasonably civilised, but this could not be said about the Civil War. Aberdeen was always on the losing side! In 1639, the city was royalist. The Earl of Montrose advanced at the head of a large force of Covenanters, allies of the English Parliament. He tricked the defenders of the city into leaving their defensive position and swept to victory, with few casualties on either side. In 1644, Covenanters were in control in Aberdeen, but the Earl had changed sides. There was a brief battle, called the Fecht o' Aberdeen or – in conventional English – the Battle of Justice Mills. Montrose had promised his army, composed largely of Irish Catholics, that they could do as they pleased if they won. There followed several days of murder, abduction and theft. This was one of the worst atrocities of the Civil War in Great Britain. The local historian, Simon Spalding, counted 120 bodies in the city and its environs.

In the same decade, in Ireland, the English New Model Army committed the massacres of Drogheda and Wexford. While Irish politicians and spokesmen polish the memory of these dreadful events, often using them in arguments about today's situation, we, in Aberdeen, have forgotten ours.

The Civil War, as far as it affected Aberdeen, reversed the Marxist view of history repeating itself. The farce came first, followed by the tragedy. King's reputation for papist sympathies did not prevent the Puritan officers of the New Model Army stationed in Aberdeen in the 1650s from donating money for an extension to the college. Equally at the Restoration, three years after his death, the Lord Protector's body may have been dug up and hanged but the building at the back of the chapel is called Cromwell's Tower to this day.

THE MARKET CROSS 1892 A90302

The very grand cross is still where it was in this view. The railings and lamps have gone, but similar lamps have recently been installed along the Castlegate. All the buildings shown here still stand. Puritans disapproved of crosses and removed them from market places. After the Restoration, Aberdeen decided that a new Market Cross was needed, although it was 1686 before it was erected. It was worth awaiting, as it is a splendid edifice, decorated with portraits of the Stuart kings and the one tragic Queen of Scots and topped by a long column with, at its summit, the unicorn, holding a shield displaying the lion rampant, the royal beast of Scotland.

It has presided over the changing fortunes of the Castlegate for more than three centuries, during which time it has seen the market expand as the city grew more prosperous and populous, and then contract as retailing retreated inside into shops. It has seen the markets removed altogether and the trams running round it, till they also were removed. It has been used as the city's first post office, till increasing literacy demanded bigger premises. Important proclamations were made from it, with the members of the town council sitting on the raised platform inside. It has been shifted to other parts of the Castlegate and it has been ignored as the centre of commercial activity moved westward to the new streets. It has recently heard the noise of modern electronic sound equipment, as the official ceremonies to bring in a New Year are held.

THE MARKET CROSS, DETAIL SHOWING THE ROYAL ARMS 1892 A90302x

Left to right: The royal arms, showing England, France, Ireland and Scotland. King James VII. King Charles II. Around the frieze, all the Stuart monarchs from James I (1424-37) are portrayed, as are the city's arms.

The Advocates in Aberdeen

Lawyers who plead cases in the High Courts of Scotland are called advocates. Just as no English solicitor would call himself a barrister, no Scottish solicitor would call himself an advocate except in Aberdeen. Here, any solicitor can join the Society of Advocates. The name is ancient, dating at least from the 17th century and was confirmed by a royal charter in 1774. Objections by the Edinburgh establishment cannot succeed against such authority.

In 1707, the Scottish MP's, many of them bribed with English money, voted for the 'Incorporating Union' and thus ended Scotlands independence, such as it was. In Aberdeen, as elsewhere, the Union was unpopular, but there was little open hostility here, as people knew that there was nothing they could do about it.

Compared to the massacre of 1644, the Jacobite Rebellions caused only minor problems. The '15 started on Deeside and many in the city were sympathetic to the Jacobite cause. The British government, in any case, removed all the fire-arms from the city, leaving the rebels in unchallenged control. With the failure of the rebellion, the Jacobite burgesses were expelled from the guild. But, when the '45 started, the government, in the person of General Cope, again removed all of the city's weapons, leaving the rebels in control again. The reason given was their fear of the weapons falling into rebel hands, but this then actually happened when the general was defeated at Prestonpans!

When the rebels won a small battle at Inverury, fifteen miles to the north of Aberdeen, they dragged Provost Morison, a Hanoverian, out to drink a toast to King James VIII. When he refused, they attempted to pour the wine into his mouth, but most of it spilt from his chin to his jacket. He earned the title 'Provost Positive' for this display of courage.

Late in the year, as the Jacobites were forced to retreat, the British army, commanded by the Duke of Cumberland, arrived. Although most Aberdonians supported the Hanoverian cause, these troops behaved as an army of occupation. Cumberland and other generals took over people's houses and stole many of their possessions. Virtually everyone was pleased to see them march away early in 1746. The overwhelming victory of Cumberland's army at Culloden on 16 April 1745 destroyed the Jacobites totally.

Provost Positive, restored to power in 1746, continued to live up to his name. The citizens were ordered to display lights in their windows as a sign of support for the Hanoverian order. An officer in charge of the remaining troops had some windows broken, where he thought that his support was insufficiently displayed. The provost had him arrested, despite claims that this was way beyond his powers. He also won compensation from the government for the damage.

Culloden was to be the last pitched battle on the land of Great Britain. In the Highlands, a time of remorseless brutality followed. But elsewhere, the peace ensured the development of both the economy and intellect. Like other cities, Aberdeen expanded and innovated, looking to the future.

Even in the early 17th century, important developments in the city's facilities were made. A quayside was built out in the Inches, the muddy area behind it filled in to extend the land. Vessels could lie at the quay, loading and discharging cargo without being stranded on the mud as

17 CASTLEGATE 1892 A90302z

17 Castlegate was built in the 1760s. The house is in Loanhead granite, and this photograph shows the eaves courses, designed to prevent rainwater washing down the wall and leeching out the mortar. In the next century, industrial production made cast-iron gutters cheaper and they were more effective at this task.

the tide ebbed. Streets were laid out on the reclaimed land with warehouses and other buildings adding to the assets of the port.

With peace secure after 1746, more ambitious plans were made. The steep rise from the shore to the Castlehill, once an advantage, was now just an obstruction. But with the extension of the land, it was possible to lay out a road straight from the quay to the Castlegate, the marketplace of Aberdeen. To start construction, a house on the Castlegate

had to be bought and demolished. This house had belonged to the Earls Marischal, the last of whom had been disgraced because of his support for the '15 rebellion. Indeed he had suffered attainder, losing all his possessions, including his title. Normally, this would mean that no-one would want to admit having anything to do with the family. But their prestige in Aberdeen was sky high, because they had founded the Toon's College. The new street, laid out in 1767, was named Marischal Street.

The two centres of commerce were directly connected at last. The street had to be carried on a viaduct all of its length. Halfway along, it strode over Virginia Street, laid along the old natural shoreline. This was probably the first example anywhere of the urban flyover.

BRICK GABLE, MARKET CROSS 1892 A90302v

Before the golden age of granite, brick was often used for gables, even in a building right in the middle of the city. This is a very early form of flats, possibly built about 1775. Some remnants of even older buildings remain at the back.

The bridge did its work for two centuries, carrying traffic of a scale unimaginable to its builders. At the end of this period, the council wanted to widen Virginia Street. They just demolished the old bridge, replacing it with a cheap and nasty lump of concrete.

The construction of Marischal Street gave a great boost to what was to become Aberdeen's most prominent characteristic - granite buildings. Granite is formed in the Earth's mantle, where temperature and pressure are so great that rock behaves as a liquid. Granite is harder than most rocks at the surface, which means that it is more expensive to work. It is also fairly unusual. Scotland's other cities are all built of sandstone, because that is the natural rock on which they sit. In medieval times, towns were built mainly of timber. So masons were few in number and moved from place to place, as their skills were required for the building of major projects, such as cathedrals and castles. Few of them would have worked granite. Even in the north-east, such masonry as was built often used imported freestone, as was the case with King's College in 1500 and even with the West Kirk of St Nicholas in 1751. St Machar's was a real exception. But as new building became more frequent, the local stone became more attractive, because large quantities of heavy, bulky material, such as stone for building, could not easily be transported. The opening of the quarries at Loanhead, only about a mile from Aberdeen, produced a supply of granite, consistent in strength and appearance. Both the viaduct and the houses along Marischal Street were built of Loanhead granite.

Aberdeen then really became the Granite City.

THE ALBERT MEMORIAL c1870 SA000007 (Courtesy of University of St Andrews Library)

Peace is just what is required for trade, especially overseas trade. To carry the goods to be traded, ships are needed. Shipbuilding, already established before the 18th century, greatly expanded. Merchants from Aberdeen had long gone into country areas to distribute wool, which was then knitted, especially into stockings, by cottars' wives. As peace was now secure, some merchants started to build mills in which first the spinning, but, later also the weaving, was done on an industrial scale. Mills were also built to work cotton and linen.

As Aberdeen set out to become a industrial city, joining such places as Glasgow and Birmingham in their drive to achieve something entirely new, we got nothing but obstruction from the government. They imposed a tax on coal, that most essential element in industrial development, payable only to the north of a point between Arbroath and Montrose. The Scottish Executive of the 21st century has revived this attitude, giving Aberdeen the lowest per capita grant in Scotland. Glasgow's poverty and Edinburgh's wealth both seem to entitle them to privileged positions.

The large numbers of workers needed in the shipyards and mills increased the population of the city and the traditional trades of bakers, fleshers and tailors increased

Did you know?

The Anglican church in the USA originates in Aberdeen. English colonies were all part of the London diocese. After American independence, Anglicans there wanted their own bishops. In the Anglican church, only a bishop can consecrate another bishop. When Connecticut sent Samuel Seabury to England for consecration, the bishops refused, regarding him as a rebel. The Scottish church had been disestablished for supporting James VII. On 14 November 1784, Seabury was consecrated the first overseas bishop of the Anglican Communion by three Scottish bishops. Anglicans from all over the world came to Aberdeen to celebrate his bicentenary in 1984.

to supply their new customers, but the built-up area hardly expanded. The city was becoming overcrowded.

In 1794 the town council decided to call a large public meeting to discuss plans for the complete transformation of the city. As a tiny, unrepresentative body, the council felt that it could not go ahead with so grand and expensive a project without the agreement of the wider community. It was in the very last year of the century that work began.

CHAPTER THREE

The Great Century: the City Triumphant

REGENT'S QUAY 1878   SA000001 (Courtesy of University of St Andrews Library)

TO THE WEST OF ABERDEEN, the deep, steep glen of the Den Burn was a barrier to expansion. On the other side lay a large expanse of fairly flat land, well drained, with burn on either side. It was the ideal place to build a modern city.

The plan for access was audacious in the extreme. Part of the city centre to the west of the Castlegate would be demolished and the top of St Catherine's Hill removed. A new street was to be laid out, almost a mile long, carried on a viaduct for nearly half of its length. The viaduct would rise to carry the street to a level higher than the east bank of the burn so that a bridge over the glen would give access to the higher west bank and the land beyond. In 1801, just as this work was starting, the parliaments of Great Britain and Ireland were united. The new street was called Union Street.

This was not all. Another new street would

THE SOUTH BRIDGE 2005 A90704k (Norman Miller)

Carrying Holburn Street over the Ferryhill Burn, South Bridge is an essential part of the great developments of the early 19th century. It gets no recognition from the bureaucracy.

be laid out northwards from the Castlegate, reasonably straight and level, to the bank of the River Don, where a new bridge would carry it to the main road to Buchan. This would avoid the old steep and twisting road over the top of the ridges from the royal burgh to Old Aberdeen and the even more difficult road to the Brig o' Balgownie. This was to be called King Street.

To reach the Brig o' Dee and the main road south, a third street would go from the West End of Union Street, crossing the Ferryhill Burn on a short viaduct. This was to become Holburn Street.

The design of the bridge to carry the street across the Den Burn was chosen by public competition, as was usual then and now. But when it came to constructing this bridge, it was found that it just could not be done, because the designer had not taken the levels of the ground accurately. So Thomas Fletcher, a local man who had been appointed superintendent of works, designed a quite different structure. It was the best thing that could have happened. Fletcher's bridge strode across the glen in a single magnificent arch of 130 feet, the widest granite span in the world.

As the new street extended half a mile beyond the old built-up area and a section of the town centre had been demolished, there were many opportunities for designing new buildings. These would be really grand buildings, showing the wealth and sophistication of a city that was launching itself into a new century.

Cometh the hour, cometh the men!

Did you know?

Aberdeen is the only Scottish local authority to have declared itself bankrupt! This was in 1821. It is believed that the city was not really bankrupt, but simply did not want to pay its debts, when the main expenses of laying out Union Street had been incurred. The council believed that, as new building went ahead, money would pour into the council's coffers. This duly happened and the bankruptcy was discharged in 1828. Some suggest that Aberdeen's reputation for meanness dates from this manoeuvre, but this is clearly nonsense. We were always mean - and always proud of it!

THE HINGE OF THE CITY AND TENEMENT 2005 A90723k (Norman Miller)

This shows the bank designed by Archibald Simpson (1839), topped with a statue of Demeter, and a large block of houses by John Smith (c1810), showing Smith's characteristic recessed, curved corner.

Aberdeen is fortunate indeed that two of her own sons were there to do this work. John Smith (1781-1852), was one. He was Fletcher's deputy, taking over Fletcher's job when he retired in 1807 on the completion of the main structural work, and he was to become the first city architect. Smith and Archibald Simpson (1790-1847) designed much of the new centre of the city. Even more fortunately, most of their buildings survive to this day.

UNION BUILDINGS
1892 A90301v

Union Buildings were designed by Archibald Simpson (1822). The tall windows between the pilasters on the first and second storeys were to light the reading room of the Atheneum, a gentlemen's club. Later, this was to be a restaurant. Following a fire in 1973, this was rebuilt as two conventional storeys. The front to Union Street is dramatically austere, in the Aberdonian manner.

The predominant architectural style of the time was neo-classical. It is restrained, balanced and austere. In Aberdeen, granite was now available from new deep quarries, especially Rubislaw, about a mile to the west of the end of Union Street. It produced pale blue granite of great hardness and consistency. So much of the city was built of Rubislaw granite that the quarry was to become the largest artificial hole in Europe. Granite is hard, it is uncommon and it sparkles in the sunshine. It has no need of elaborate ornamentation. The material is impressive enough in itself. Aberdeen has no mineral wealth other than the granite. It is remote from the main industrial and commercial centres and the climate, in winter, is harsh. It was the genius of Smith and Simpson to design buildings of exceptional severity, so appropriate for both the material and the social context.

The Old Urban Myth about Union Street

One council faction wanted a magnificent boulevard. Another wanted the new street merely to be wider than the existing ones. This miserable, stingy faction won. When the surveyors marked out the line of the new street, the others, rising in the middle of the night, shifted the posts to the positions needed for the boulevard. Next morning, the navvies dug out the basis of the street as marked by the posts. The mean faction could hardly complain about the undermining of democratic decisions. The councillors of the time met every year and elected themselves back on to the council.

REGENT'S QUAY 1878 SA000001 (Courtesy of University of St Andrews Library)

Sailing vessels are seen here at Regent's Quay. They were still dominant well into the 19th century.

King Street only made any sense if there was to be a bridge over the Don at its northern end. From 1827 to 1830, a bridge of five round granite arches was built, at no cost to local tax-payers. This was possible because in 1605 Sir Alexander Hay had left a bequest for the maintenance of the Old Bridge and this, by the careful husbandry of the town council, had grown to such an extent that it provided the £26,000 needed

for the construction of the new. The original width was doubled in 1958.

It was also decided that the Dee needed a second bridge. Here, the frontiers of technology were employed. The Dee flowed through a narrow gap at Craig Lug (Rocky Ear), where a suspension bridge was built in 1829. This was the lowest point on the Dee where any kind of bridge was possible at the time. It joined the city to Nigg parish.

THE SUSPENSION BRIDGE c1885 A90303

The narrowing of the river at this point shows clearly why the bridge was built here. By the time this photograph was taken, the muddy Inches were entirely reclaimed and the growing city occupies all of the horizon. Officially the Wellington Suspension Bridge, it has always been called locally, the Chain Brig.

John Smith, Aberdeen's first city architect, designed both these bridges, working with Captain Samuel Brown in the case of the Chain Brig.

The shipyard of Alexander Hall and Co had been established in 1790. In the 1830s, William, one of the founder's sons, conducted experiments in which he made models of ships of different shapes, and pulled them across water in a tank to see which was fastest and most stable. As a result, this yard built 'Scottish Maid' in 1839, her very sharp bow letting her cut through the water at great speed. She was the first of the Scottish clippers.

Soon Hall's and other Aberdeen yards were building larger clippers, establishing a reputation for excellence. With their 'Extreme Aberdeen Bow', the clippers were the fastest vessels on the sea and were much prized, especially for the Tea trade from China. Clippers would race all the way across the world to bring back the first of the new season's tea. The first cargo to reach London would command a handsome bonus from the tea merchants.

The fastest of all clippers was 'Thermopylae', built by Walter Hood's yard in Torry, on the south bank of the Dee, in 1859. The now well-known 'Cutty Sark' was built at Dumbarton ten years later, specifically to race against 'Thermopylae'. The older vessel won the race. But 1869 also saw the opening of the Suez Canal. Sailing ships had to be towed through the canal and could no longer compete with the steam ships on the China trade. But clippers and other sailing vessels still made the journey to and from Australia till the end of the century.

The yards were soon building steamships as well. The engines were made locally. Expertise in this field had been built up in connection with the engines in the mills, but was greatly enhanced with the coming of the marine engine. Soon general engineering firms were making all sorts of machinery, both for local

consumption and for export world-wide.

Throughout the 19th century, with growth in industry, and therefore in population, the city needed to expand further. The triumphant success of the long viaduct of Union Street led to other viaduct streets. Market Street was built in 1839. It gave access from the new main street to the harbour and to the New Market, a large covered area where the butchers, in particular, were housed to take this trade out of the open stalls on the Castlegate. Bridge Street followed in the 1860s and the Rosemount and Denburn viaducts of the 1880s gave access to Rosemount, another desirable development area to the north.

Aberdeen did not have to wait for the 20th century to know about streets in the sky. We built ours in the 18th and 19th and not as anonymous concrete monstrosities, but as the unique, austere and durable Granite City. The

From a compact site in the middle of Aberdeen, this company sent machinery all over the world. As this advert suggests, they specialised in food processing plant.

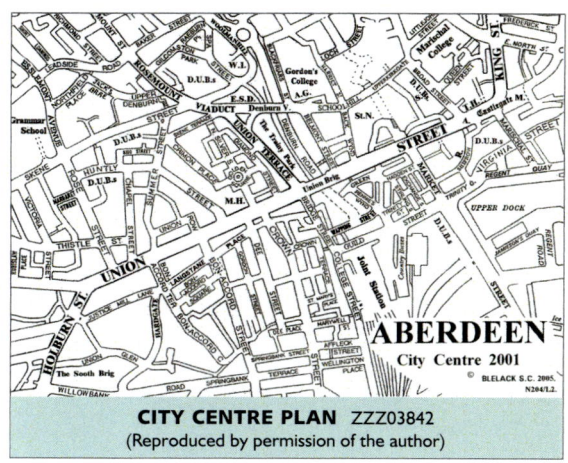

CITY CENTRE PLAN ZZZ03842
(Reproduced by permission of the author)

The modern city is still based on the viaduct streets of the 18th and 19th centuries.

buildings on the main streets were faced with what the masons called 'esslar', pronounced 'AIS-lar'. ('ashlar' in the Queen's English.) The edges of the blocks are cut precisely straight, so that they fit tightly together, horizontally and vertically. The mortar between the stones is hardly visible. Careful selection of the best stones for the front of the buildings results in the whole public face looking as if it had been cut from the same stone.

Prince Albert's favourite painter, William Dyce (1806 - 1869) was born in Aberdeen and educated at the Grammar School and Marischal College. He left for London as a young man and quickly established a reputation as an artist. A high-church Anglican, many of his paintings were of traditional religious subjects, although he also painted landscapes and portraits. On a visit to Italy, he met and was greatly influenced by the German Nazarene artist, Overbeck, whose ideas were to inspire the Pre-Raphaelite

painters later in the century. Dyce became Superintendent of the Design Schools in London in 1837 and was to be a major figure in the field of formal art education. He was commissioned to paint large frescoes in the Robing Room of the Palace of Westminster, when it was rebuilt, after fire destroyed much of the old building in 1834. This room is where the monarch dresses in full ceremonial attire before delivering the Queen's Speech to Parliament. He died before he could complete this task. The architect Charles Barry and the interior designer Augustus Pugin also died while the work was continuing. Aberdeen Art Gallery has forty of his works and others are to be found in major galleries in London. Aberdeen College has recently named its training restaurant after him. We are left to wonder what the man would have made of such an honour!

THE WATER HOUSE 2005 A90711k (Norman Miller)

The Water House was designed by John Smith (1830). The top storey was a cistern, supplying water to the city, all of which was below it at this time. No longer required in the more sophisticated days at the end of the century, it became what it had always appeared to be, a rather superior tenement.

50 QUEEN'S ROAD 2005 A90718k (Norman Miller)

This shows a particularly grand house in Aberdeen's grandest street, constructed for the leading Victorian builder John Morgan.

The railway reached Aberdeen in 1850. It was then possible to go from the city to London in only one day. Local companies built lines to the north and west. By the end of the century, the north-east was covered in branch lines, all belonging to the Aberdeen-based Great North of Scotland Railway. The city could now bring in the raw materials and fuel for industry and agriculture and export the products of both. People were free to travel as never before. But not only ordinary people: Queen Victoria had her new home at Balmoral. The double-headed royal train was a familiar sight on Royal Deeside from the 1850s till the 1960s.

Alexander Anderson (1802-1887), son of the parish minister at Strichen, was educated at the Grammar School and Marischal College. His profession was the law. He used his skills to help establish several companies, some of which were to play a significant role in the developing economy of the city and the whole of the north-east. Among these companies were the Great North of Scotland Railway, the North of Scotland Bank and the North of Scotland Fire and Life Assurance

Company. These were the days in which a group of local business and professional men could found a bank!

Anderson's activities were such that, at a certain point, he felt it best to fade from his prominent position. But if he had broken the rules, he had been careful enough not to get caught. Re-emerging into the spotlight in 1859, he was elected to the town council. The Local Government Reform Act of 1833 had started to open up councils to a wider electorate. He was immediately elected as provost, which brought complaints from some members. So Anderson resigned his seat, stood again and won again. He was then unchallengeable!

THE NORTH OF SCOTLAND BANK HEADQUARTERS AND MARKET CROSS c1905 A90320 (Detail)

The North of Scotland Bank Headquarters, designed by Archibald Simpson (1839). Called the Hinge of the City, because of its prominent position, it is a brilliant solution to the problem - for neo-classical architecture - of an irregular angle between the streets. The curving entrance unites what are effectively two buildings, one on each street. The columns are Corinthian, unusual in Aberdeen. The statue is of Demeter, goddess of plenty, by James Giles. Like many others, this building is now a public house.

Thus began the time of Aberdeen's greatest-ever civic head. His most important contribution was the scheme for a water supply, starting at Invercannie, over twenty miles from the city. The validity of this plan, which was seen by some at the time as extravagant, is best demonstrated by the fact that most of the city's water still comes from Invercannie, despite the enormous increase in the quantities consumed. Boldness and vision paid handsome dividends, as was often to be the case with Victorian municipal authorities. He supervised the continued development of the harbour. He arranged the rebuilding of the grammar school on what we would now call a green-field site, which is now, of course, in the middle of the city. The architect of the new school was James Matthews, who was himself to become provost in 1883.

Provost Anderson was also one of the first to bring Queen Victoria out of the secluded widowhood into which she had retreated on the death of Prince Albert. He realised that the only public duty she would agree to perform would be to unveil a statue of the Prince. The statue was made and set up on Union Street. The Queen came to perform the ceremony and she then knighted Provost Anderson. Not only that, she said, 'My Lord Provost!' From that time, the civic head of Aberdeen has been the Lord Provost. He was the first of many to be knighted for services to the city.

Sir Alexander was provost from 1859 until 1865. He was later to be appointed as the civic head of Fraserburgh, where he also supervised improvements to the harbour.

THE QUEEN'S MONUMENT c1870 SA000008
(Courtesy of St Andrews University Library)

This statue of Queen Victoria stands in the centre of her royal burgh. This marble statue was soon considered too delicate for the urban atmosphere and was replaced by one in bronze. It has now been moved to Queen's Cross, facing westwards to Balmoral. The marble statue now stands at the back of the main lobby of the Town House, facing all the visitors who enter.

He was a major figure in the City of Aberdeen Land Association, a Victorian property developing company. It still exists, now called 'CALA Homes'.

Contemporary with Sir Alexander was Sir John Anderson (1814-1886). They shared a surname and both were knighted, but there the resemblance ended. John was born into a working-class family in a village just north of Aberdeen, which would later be called Woodside. He became an apprentice at Woodside Works, a mill in which cotton was spun, woven and printed. He would walk the two miles into the city in the evening to attend a class at the Mechanics' Institute and then walk back and still be up in time to start work early the next morning. On finishing his apprenticeship he, like many others, went south, finding work in Manchester and London. Finally he was recommended to the Royal Arsenal, where he introduced many improvements. He suggested that the Arsenal manufacture rifles for the British Army, rather than rely on private armourers. He studied Belgian and American mechanised processes for this and then introduced them, easily beating the largely manual systems of the old suppliers in price and speed of delivery. He equipped a ship as a floating workshop to go to the Crimea. In retirement, he was much in demand as a judge of machinery at international exhibitions. He was not only knighted by Queen Victoria, but was awarded similar honours by the French and the Austrians.

WINDMILL BRAE 2005 A90/25k (Norman Miller)

After fifty years of government by mindless modernisers, it is not easy to find a granite street in the Granite City now. Here, appropriately, the old main road south is still in causeway setts (pronounced 'Kas-aiz' in Doric) while the new (1860s) viaduct of Bridge Street can be seen striding across the old road.

The Doric

For centuries, ordinary folk in Aberdeen and the north-east spoke an Anglo-Saxon dialect called Doric. With its implications of being rural and unsophisticated, the term 'Doric' probably started as an insult, but, as often happens, the victim adopted it as a sign that he was not intimidated by the supposed superiority of the detractor. Despised for centuries and suppressed with contempt and physical violence at schools, little remains in today's speech. An effort is now being made to teach Doric poetry and stories at some schools and there is a Doric festival every year.

He did not forget his days in Woodside and the benefits he had obtained from the schools and debating societies that flourished there. He donated a fund to provide a prize of £2 each year for the dux (top pupil) of Woodside School. But his main project was to create a library open to all the people of his birthplace. He returned in 1881 to hand over his gift. Woodside was now a burgh and the council organised a splendid festival, with a parade along the main street and a feast for the whole population. The library was first

THE SIR JOHN ANDERSON LIBRARY AT WOODSIDE 2005   A90702k (Norman Miller)

Still in use as a branch library, an extension at the back now houses the city library's collection of newspapers, an invaluable historical asset.

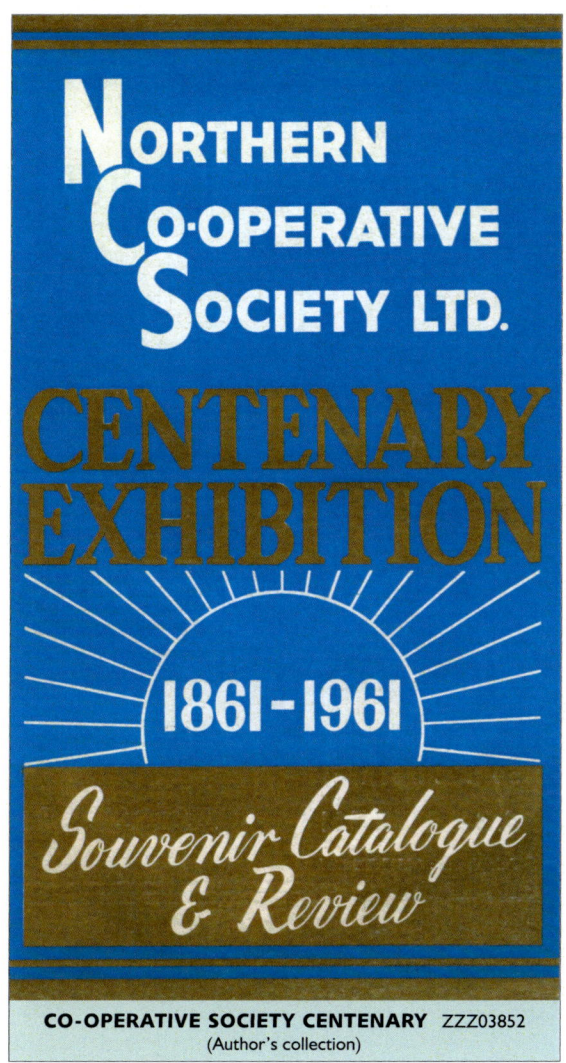

CO-OPERATIVE SOCIETY CENTENARY ZZZ03852
(Author's collection)

From small beginnings in 1861, the 'Co-opie' was to become the largest retailer in the north-east, with branches all over the city and in nearby towns and a large and loyal customer base. Its sudden collapse into bankruptcy has never been satisfactorily explained.

housed in the school, but Sir John realised that it required a building of its own. He took out a feu (a perpetual lease at a fixed rent) on land near the school and supervised the design of the new library, a beautiful little building in granite esslar, which could easily be mistaken for a kirk. Sadly, he never saw it, as he was too ill to come to the opening in 1883. His project lives on as the Sir John Anderson branch of the public library of Aberdeen.

Ironically, certain similarities appeared after the deaths of these two very different men. Sir Alexander's son, Andrew, donated his father's books to form the basis of the Library at Strichen. Late in the 19th century, a new road was laid out at the west end of Woodside. This was called Anderson Road, after Sir John. In the 1920s, a road was laid out as a western bypass of Aberdeen. It was called Anderson Drive, after Sir Alexander.

If the 19th century was the century of dramatic change in Aberdeen, the 1870s were a decade of particular intensive change. The Education (Scotland) Act (1872) compelled all children to attend school. This clearly, changed the lives of children, opening up all sorts of possibilities for them. It also meant that many new school buildings were required. The School Board started building in 1876. Most schools were solid, impressive but fairly plain buildings in granite esslar. One of the first, Causewayend (pronounced CASS-ai-AIN in the Doric) was, about twenty years later, given an extension that included a tower, said to be adapted from the one at Balmoral, giving a very grand appearance to a school in one of the poorest areas of the city.

ST MARY'S ROMAN CATHOLIC CATHEDRAL 1889
SA000032 (Courtesy of University of St Andrews Library)

This was Aberdeen's third cathedral, the second being the Anglican St Andrew's in King Street. St Mary's was designed by William Ellis, whose many kirks gave him his nickname, 'Holy Ellis'. The spire was added, by his partner Robert Wilson in 1877, celebrating the achievement of cathedral status.

Schools also need teachers. This necessitates an increased provision of higher education. As a generation goes through the schools, more of them are ready to go into professional work and those in manual jobs are able routinely to do more sophisticated work. They learn more about the materials with which they work, with the help of classes run by the Mechanics' Institute. Later the Trades College, started by the Kirk as part of its commitment to education, took responsibility for this work.

GORDON'S COLLEGE 1889   SA000031 (Detail)
(Courtesy of University of St Andrews Library)

This shows the 'Auld Hoos', the original building of 1731, designed by William Adam. The school was founded by Robert Gordon (1665-1732), an Aberdeen merchant, for the education of orphaned boys, those called Gordon having first preference. The building was complete by 1739, but its careful founder had specified that no pupils should be taken till the investments were enough to sustain the future of the undertaking. Schooling started in 1750, making it much the oldest private school in the city. Like its great rival, the Grammar School, it is now coeducational.

Aberdeen had always been a centre for professional services to the rural areas as well as its own population. From the 1870s, this aspect of work became more important. A virtuous cycle of expanding educational attainment had been started. The increased sophistication of society, plus the rising population of the city required more legal and financial services, more record keeping and better welfare provision. This was possible because of better educational standards. The nature of work changed significantly and social attitudes changed with it.

It was in the 1870s that the harbour was completed. The River Dee was confined to a channel at the southern edge of the formerly wide Inches. Two long docks were built, with quaysides and warehouses for handling the cargoes, and water deep enough to keep the vessels floating even at low tide. Breakwaters were built further out into the sea, protecting the harbour from even the fiercest storms and causing a powerful scour that largely stopped the harbour from being silted. Railway lines were laid along the quays, allowing exports from and imports to all over the north-east to be handled.

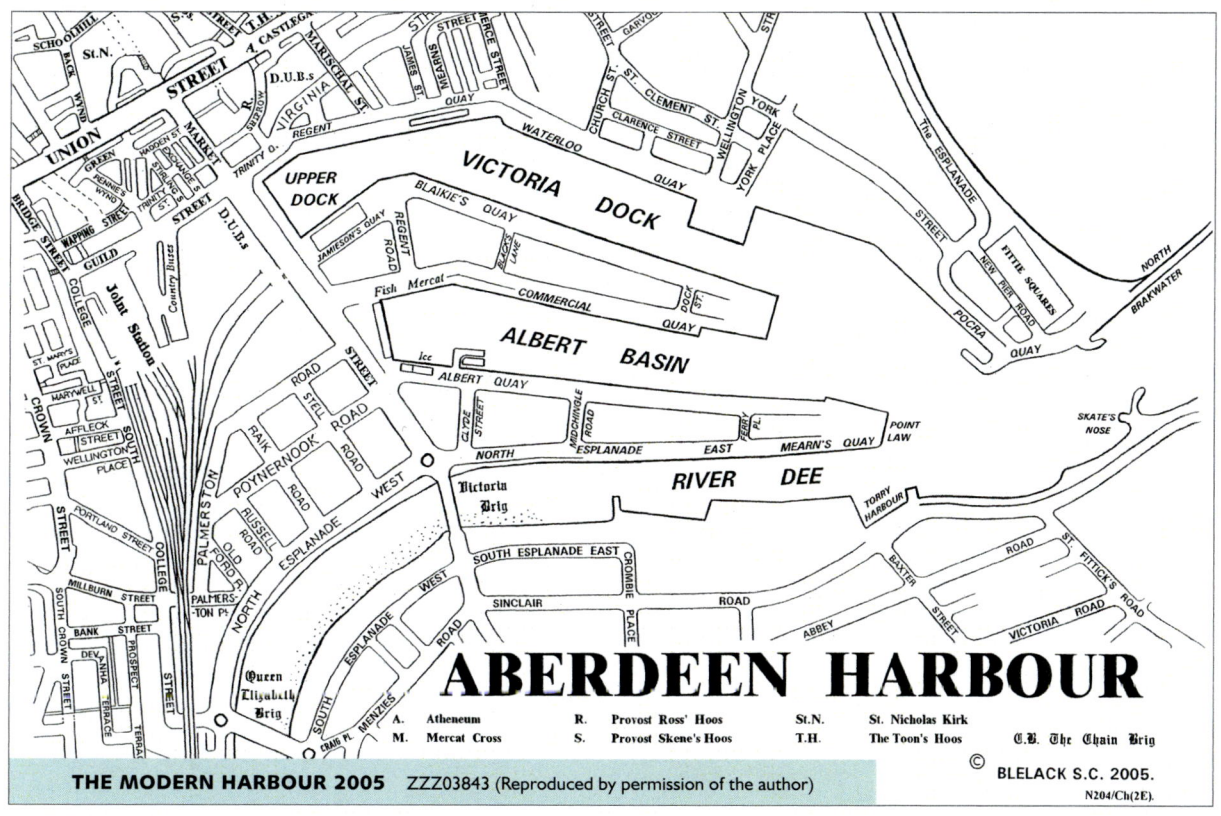

THE MODERN HARBOUR 2005 ZZZ03843 (Reproduced by permission of the author)

This modern harbour is a great contrast to the natural Inches beside which the people started to settle centuries ago.

DOCKSIDE WAREHOUSE 2005 A90716k (Norman Miller)

The initials of the Shore Porters' Society are carried on the gablet. This is the second oldest commercial company in the world, in existence since at least 1498. Aberdeen Harbour Board is the oldest! The date plaque of 1861 is the first of a long series of such plaques in the city.

In 1874, the trams arrived. A private company, the Aberdeen District Tramways, laid two lines along the main streets, Union Street and George Street. The former proceeded to the West End, where people were rich enough to afford the fares! Each tram was drawn by a pair of horses. The new service, with only a few teething problems, quickly became popular. In the next few years, the routes were extended, and a new one laid. Large numbers of people were soon using the trams regularly.

Along with the trams come the tenements.

The working classes, able to travel by tram, no longer have to live close to the workplace. This allows greater freedom of choice in work and it often results in better health, as families go to live in less polluted places at the edge of the city. There were, of course, those who lived by providing such housing for rent. They were known in Aberdeen as 'lairdies'.

Large blocks divided into flats had been built for some time, but it was from the 1870s that the great expansion of the tenements took place. At first, they were often built in coursed rubble, the description of stones only

1889 TENEMENTS PHOTOGRAPHED IN 2005 A90714k (Norman Miller)

Tenements in granite esslar swing round from Holburn Street into Ashvale Place, just above the South Bridge.

roughly cut to the same size. Indeed, until the 1840s, it was common even for rather genteel terraces for the better off to be built thus, if they were outside the main streets in the centre of the city. Even so, the hard, solid local stone was used for even the humblest of the tenements. Granite was triumphant. The quarries could scarcely supply all the stone that was needed and many small quarries opened to compete with Rubislaw.

The next decades up till the First World War saw the golden age of granite. Now the added expense of cutting this hard stone did not matter. Nearly everything was built of it: grand villas for the wealthy, neat terraces for the reasonably prosperous, tenements for the working classes, kirks of all denominations, municipal buildings, schools, banks and even industrial buildings. Indeed the later tenements were built in precise granite esslar, dramatically impressive in their plain severity. Villas and terraces in the West End had bow windows and cornices with very flat surfaces cut with the mason's axe contrasting with bulging rusticated stones in between. Even the Model Lodging House, for the accommodation of the poorest of citizens, was built in granite.

The expansion of the city brought a concentration of people and pollution. Open spaces were needed to act as lungs. Aberdeen's first public park was the small, but very central, Union Terrace Gardens, stretching north from Union Bridge along the west bank of the Den Burn, which, steeper and higher than the east bank, was unsuitable for building. The Burn was by this time underground, with the railway following its course, connecting the lines from north and south of the city. The gardens were to be known popularly as the 'Trainy Park'.

UNION TERRACE GARDENS c1900 A90311

The city's first public park already has mature trees by this time. Education, Salvation and Damnation preside over this pleasant scene.

THE MODELLER 2005 A90703k (Norman Miller)

Built all over the country to a plan or model, the model lodging houses are instantly recognisable. Aberdeen's has the corbie (crow) step gables of the Scottish Baronial style and the city's coat of arms proudly displayed on the centre gablet. It has been converted into modern flats.

When the Denburn Viaduct was built at the north end of the gardens, they remained an oasis of verdure in the centre of the built-up area. Trees grew into forest giants, contrasting pleasantly with their urban surroundings, pale and optimistic in spring, full and lively in summer, colourful in autumn and stark in winter. In the 20th century, planners have made several attempts to replace this priceless asset with a multi-storey car park. They have not succeeded, but no doubt they will try again. Later in the same decade, the Victoria Park was situated towards the west of the urban area. This developed into a quiet, leafy place, most suitable for the very young and the elderly. The later Westburn Park, just over the road, is open for more boisterous pursuits.

The Prestige of Granite

When, in 1867, Edinburgh architects Peddie and Kinnear won the contract to design a new Town House, they thought of building it in freestone. It was made clear to the council that this would not be acceptable. John Fife, owner of Kemnay Quarry, twenty miles west of Aberdeen, guaranteed to supply enough of the best quality granite for the job.

In 1872, Rubislaw Kirk, designed to serve the increasing population of the West End, was built - in freestone. This so offended the pioneer photographer George Washington Wilson, whose house was on the opposite side of Queen's Cross from the Kirk, that he bought the one remaining corner of the Cross and built a house in granite there.

THE TOWER OF THE NEW TOWN HOUSE 1892 A90301x

The tower of the new Town House has turrets at all four corners, held up by corbels, in the Scottish Baronial style. From the middle of the century, the neo-classical was replaced by the romantic and, in Scotland, this led to a revival of the nation's great contribution to the world of architecture. But even then, the tradition of granite severity was not altogether abandoned. Aberdeen's Victorian romantic buildings are about as elaborate as other cities' classical Georgian efforts.

Men had gone to sea to catch fish for centuries. They went out at night in small open boats, paying out long lines with bated hooks. In the morning, they returned with whatever had, literally, taken the bait. Their wives sold the fish in towns or round the farms, where it was often bartered for meal, eggs and butter. The catch was necessarily small, the industry entirely local. Aberdeen had its own fishing community, called Fittie, based further from the central built-up area than the main harbour. About 1810, it was shifted right to the point of the spit that separated the harbour from the sea. The council built squares of single-storey houses, designed by John Smith. In more recent times, some residents have extended their houses in the only direction available - upwards. Some are still single-storey, others are two or even three.

Late in the 18th century a different system was pioneered by the Dutch, although British fishermen soon became the dominant force. A larger boat went further out to sea and stayed longer. A long net was paid out, held near the surface by floats to catch fish by their gills. This drift-net fishery was especially suitable for herring, great shoals of which migrate every year southwards along the east coast of Britain. The open boats needed only a boat shore, a beach on which they could be drawn up beyond the reach of the highest tides. But the herring fishery needed solid quaysides,

FISHING FLEET 1895 SA000040
(Courtesy of University of St Andrews Library)

Sail drifters leave Aberdeen harbour. Their straight stem and stern suggest that they are 'Fifies', or their German equivalent. AN is the registration code for Norderny.

with large flat areas for gutting and packing the quantities that were brought ashore. All round the coast, harbours were built to accommodate this. Aberdeen was one of the places that did so.

In 1882, a converted tug called 'Toiler' arrived in Aberdeen, with a new style of fishing. She used her powerful engines to drag a conical net, held open by a heavy wooden beam, across the sea bottom, sweeping up all the fish in its path. This was the trawl net and it brought large quantities of fish ashore. Soon purpose-built trawlers were fishing off Aberdeen. So great were the catches that an open quayside was insufficient to handle them.

The council and the Harbour Board had the foresight to build a covered fish-market in 1889. Here boxes of fish were displayed while being auctioned. The trawlers came to Aberdeen in increasing numbers. Other ports

built covered fish-markets, but trawlers are gregarious. Aberdeen had got there first. The trawlers stayed together in their new home and made Aberdeen the biggest fishing port in the world up until the First World War.

Fittie and Footdee

The name of this place appears on maps as Footdee, but it is pronounced 'Fittie' or 'Futtie'. It probably derives from an ancient holy man, St Futine. 'Footdee' is the most crass of many attempts to Anglicise everything about Aberdeen, and indeed the whole of Scotland. The low end of a river is never the foot, always the mouth. In Anglo-Saxon names, the river always comes first, as in 'Plymouth'. 'Footdee' makes no sense at all. This seems to be a case of sycophants making fools of themselves. West Lothian became 'Linlithgowshire' for a while. What chance did Fittie stand?

FISH MARKET c1900   A90316

Merchants look at the fish shortly to be auctioned. The trawler at the extreme left clearly shows her Aberdeen Fishery registration A 69 on her funnel. The fish may end up in a local kitchen or at the other end of the country.

This was great for the economy of the city. The shipyards built large numbers of trawlers, which required nets and ice to be made and provisions to be supplied. They brought back great quantities of fish, which had to be cleaned and packed in ice or salt, or smoked. Even the offal could be used to produce fertiliser. Long trains carried fish to Billingsgate in London and other big cities. 'The Fish' was to become the largest source of employment in Aberdeen.

At the start of the 19th century, ships were built of wood and powered by sail. By the end, ships were built of steel and powered by steam engines. The shipyards in Aberdeen had made the transition, and were thriving on their new work. Two of those working in the later years of the century, Hall and Co and Hall, Russell and Co were to survive till the second half of the 20th century.

Steel ships are built round frames, made of angle-bar, which define the shape of the vessel. The frames are heated in a wide furnace and bent into shape, each pair a mirror image of the other, and slightly different from the pairs on either side, as the vessel broadens from the stem (called the bow by sailors) to the midships, and then narrows again to the stern. The shell of the ship is made of steel plates. These have to be cut to size and then curved by being pressed between sets of huge rollers till they will fit on to the frames. Finally, holes are punched at the edges to allow the rivets to go through which fasten the frames and the plates together. This work is done by platers, who then hang the plates on the frames.

Riveting is done by a team of five. The heater boy keeps the rivets hot on a small portable furnace. Just before each rivet is required, he moves it on to the hottest part of the fire, then picks it up with his long tongs and throws it to where the others are working. The catcher picks it up with his tongs and pushes it through the holes in the plates. As soon as this is done, the holder-up holds a heavy hammer against the head of the rivet. All this is happening inside the vessel being built. Outside are two riveters, one on the right and one on the left. As soon as the rivet appears, they strike it alternately with their hammers until it is flat against the outer surface of the plate. They have to do this quickly, because the rivet, in contact with cold plates, loses its heat rapidly and thus becomes more difficult to compress.

SHIP-BUILDING TOOLS 2005 ZZZ03839 (Norman Miller)

Left to right: Riveter's hammer. Rivets and service bolt (used to hold the plates in place while riveting proceeds). Catcher's tongs. Spike for aligning rivet holes and key (spanner) for service bolt.

Few physical creations of man elicit such pride and affection as ships. From the middle of the 19th until well into the 20th centuries, they were built in this way, with a great deal of skill and manual effort and not a little danger to those who worked in the yards.

In 1891, Aberdeen's boundaries were extended to include the old burgh of Old Aberdeen and the new burgh of Woodside to the north and Torry, just south of the River Dee. This established the essential pattern of the city for most of the 20th century.

Old Aberdeen survived remarkably intact and continued to be the only part of the city that looked like an old town. This was largely due to the massive changes in the city at the start of the century. Fairly straight and level, King Street was a great contrast to the old road over the top of the ridge between the two burghs. The old road had to take this seemingly difficult route, because it was the only way to keep it dry. By the early 19th century, engineers knew how to put in drains that would prevent flooding on the lower route.

Being by-passed saved Old Aberdeen, which was largely left to its own devices as the industrialised world rushed by, mostly on King Street! The university expanded slowly and even the local markets continued to operate. St Machar's, technically no more than a parish kirk in the Presbyterian system, was still an important place of worship. New houses were built, mostly in granite, although the distinctive dark red Seaton brick was still produced at the start of the century just across King Street. The burgh ambled

through the century minding its on business. Even after being incorporated into the city, the old town was largely left alone. Trams eventually ran all the way along King Street to just short of the new Bridge of Don. A few houses were built on the street and, although the brickworks closed, the Seaton Pottery produced distinctive products with swirling patterns using different colours of clay.

Woodside, in complete contrast, was a little industrial town, increasingly being integrated into the city. Trams direct from the city centre ran right along its main street. But many

**THE SALVATION ARMY CITADEL
CASTLE STREET c1900** SA000003 (Detail)
(Courtesy of University of St Andrews Library)

This shows the Salvation Army Citadel, by James Soutar, 1893. The tower, it is said, was included at the behest of General Booth. It is a copy of the tower at Balmoral. The building has a deliberately military appearance, which not only effectively 'closes' Union Street, but also balances Christ's College, which has a military flavour as well, at the west end.

here opposed the annexation of their burgh, although their opinions were not thought to be of any importance by the powers that be. They insisted on getting something in return for losing their independence. They got a new bridge over the Don, Persley Bridge, built in granite from Persley Quarry and the Stewart Park.

Just across the Don was Grandholm Mill, where woollen cloth of the highest quality was produced. Remote from the big centres of population in Britain, many firms in Aberdeen specialised in making goods of such high quality that the extra costs of transport were more than outweighed by the prices that they could command. Crombie cloth, named after the owners of the mill, was in demand for military uniforms, not only for the British army, but also for that of

GRANITE VILLA 2005 A90715k (Norman Miller)

Now extended as a doctor's surgery, this was a grand house on King Street, close to King's College. Classical symmetry remains popular at the end of the 19th century. Rusticated and axed granite contrast on the face of the house.

VICTORIA BRIDGE 2005 A90726k (Norman Miller)

Built in 1881, this finally joined Torry to the city.

Russia, where they certainly know the value of the best of clothes.

In Woodside, also, was Donside Mill, where paper was made. Paper-making in the north-east started at Culter, eight miles up Deeside from the city, in 1750, after which several other mills had opened. The extension of the city boundaries brought them closer to Muggiemoss and Stoneywood. These were large works employing hundreds of people, some of whom lived within the city. In the centre of Aberdeen were the manufacturing stationers Pirie, Appleton and Company. Paper was one of Aberdeen's main industries and was to be one of the few that survived into the 21st century.

Torry included a small, old fishing village and some recent industrial and residential developments. Separated by the muddy estuary of the Dee, Torry had long been quite different from the city. With the development of the modern harbour and narrowing of the river, and the building in 1830 of the Chain Brig just west of the Inches, this isolation had been fading. But with the opening of Victoria Bridge in 1881, giving direct access from the centre of the city and the harbour, Torry was set to develop as part of Aberdeen. This does not prevent many of Torry's residents still to this day regarding themselves as scarcely being Aberdonians!

Late in this century, two institutions came into being that contributed significantly to the cultural development of the city.

GIRDLENESS LIGHTHOUSE c1900 A90323

Girdleness Lighthouse, built in 1833, was designed by Robert Stevenson, grandfather of the novelist. The bulge in the middle used to exhibit another light during the house's first years. More than just a useful structure for sailors, Girdleness is important for all Aberdonians returning home. One soldier, being flown back in 1945 after years as a prisoner of war, recalled that the English pilot said, with some excitement, that the white cliffs of Dover were visible. 'That meant nothing to me,' the soldier said. 'What I need to see is Girdleness!'

In 1885, the art gallery was opened. The finance came largely from the granite merchants, who had a particular interest in copies of the Elgin Marbles, from which apprentice monumental masons could gain inspiration. Alexander MacDonald, who devised a means of polishing granite mechanically, left his own fine collection of paintings to the Gallery. The central library of 1891 encouraged large numbers of people to take an interest in literature and learning.

The town council had taken on more responsibilities as the century progressed. The water scheme of the 1860s was followed by the laying of proper sewers. The gas works became municipal property in 1871 and electricity generation was started at the end of the century. The tramway was run by the municipality from 1897 and a start was made to converting it to electric traction. The first few council houses were built in the 1890s. The city hospital was there to cope with infections and, although the Royal Infirmary belonged to a charity, the city fathers always took a direct interest.

Rising prosperity and increasing education seemed to be laying a good foundation for the century to come.

ST NICHOLAS STREET AND QUEEN'S CORNER c1899 A90307

A new tram on the newly electrified route waits to depart for Woodside, along the single track section through the narrow St Nicholas Street. The passing loops, designed for horse trams, were so short that the large streamliners of a later era could not work on this route. This street and George Street, just beyond it, were the main shopping places for ordinary folk. Union Street had the posh shops.

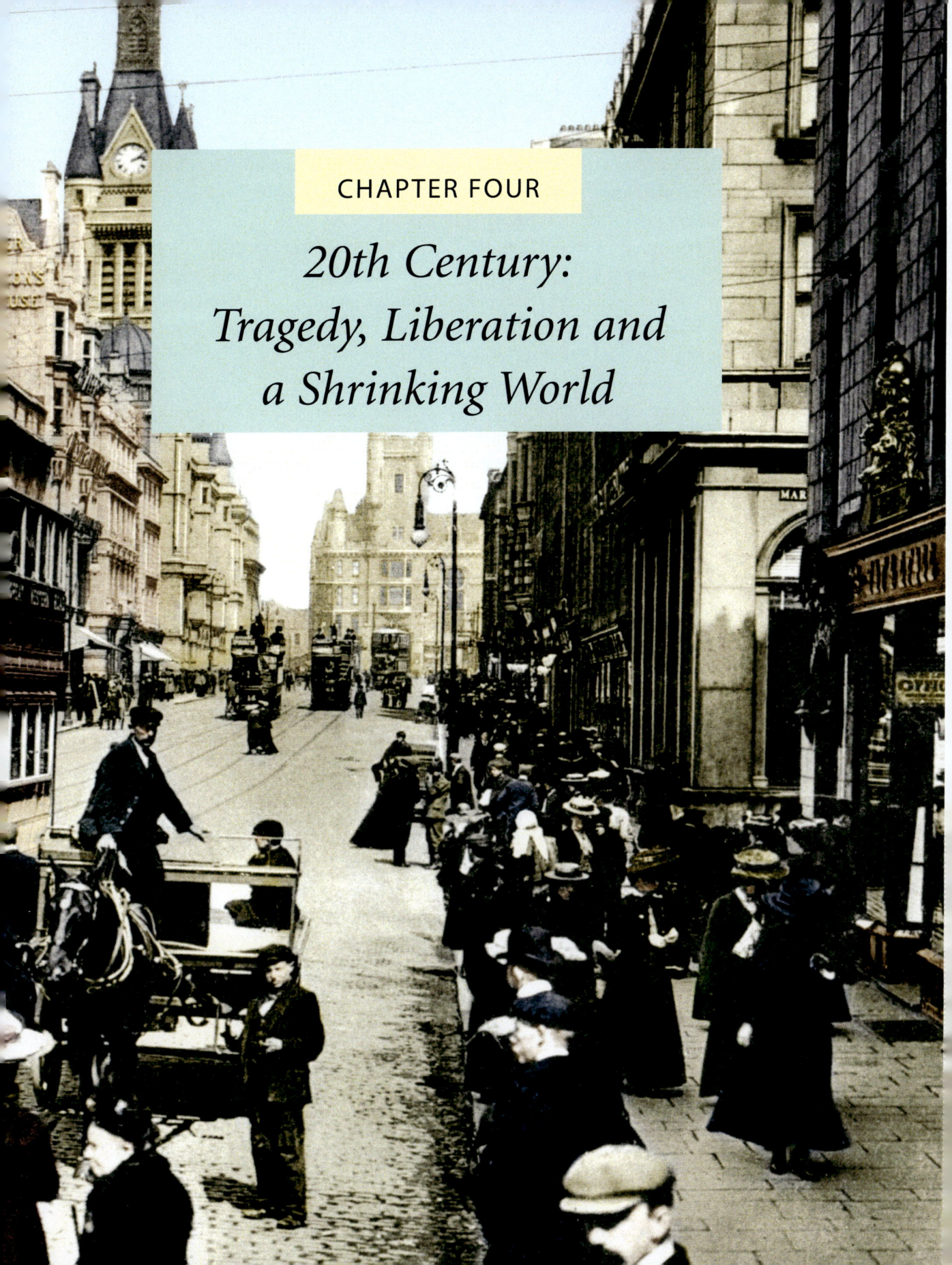

CHAPTER FOUR

20th Century: Tragedy, Liberation and a Shrinking World

FOR ITS first fourteen years the new century was much like the old. The shipyards built vessel after vessel, many for the local fishing and trading fleets, many also for export. Engineering firms sent machinery all over the world. Paper and textiles were manufactured and Miller's Chemical Works made various products, mainly for agriculture. The corporation electrified the tramway and laid down three new routes. They built a new power station to generate electricity and the number of industrial and domestic customers increased.

The population continued to rise, although more slowly. Tenements and villas were built in granite and the built-up area expanded.

Woodside grew and Torry grew quite rapidly, new streets extending further up and round the hill that now rose directly from the new, confined course of the Dee. Torry was reached by one of the new tram routes. Old Aberdeen continued to live quietly, still a real urban community going about its diverse business.

The university had started a big expansion of Marischal College late in the 19th century and went on to construct a huge new building along Broad Street, one of the original streets of the medieval city. The architect was Alexander Marshall Mackenzie (1848-1933) and he designed a fantastically elaborate front to the street, all gothic detail

THE HARBOUR 1889 SA000029 (Detail) (Courtesy of University of St Andrews Library)

By the beginning of the new century, the skyline is still dominated by the civic and the sacred, and in Aberdeen's case, the academic. Left to right: the Town House, Marischal College and the Salvation Army Citadel. No tower blocks are to be seen!

The elaborate new front to Broad Street, Aberdeen's biggest and most intricate building, is seen here. Now abandoned by the university, this part of it may soon become the town council's main administrative centre. None of the houses in the foreground survived slum clearance.

MARISCHAL COLLEGE c1900 A90318

and fussiness, with little gold pennants at the top of the many gablets. A splendid tribute to the skill and hard work of the masons, it is as well that it is the only building of its kind in Aberdeen. It is the second largest granite building in the world.

For the ceremonial opening in 1906, King Edward VII came from Balmoral in the royal train. The city was decorated with huge garlands and arches over the streets.

The king's procession from Holburn Street Station took a long route through the city, and was recorded on film, one of the very first newsreels. Lunch was served to a large company, with cigarettes on the tables, as was the usual way at this time.

Marshal Mackenzie did design many fine buildings. His Cults Free Kirk of 1915 is brilliant. Unmistakably a kirk, it is plain and unassuming, as is particularly right for a Presbyterian building and for granite. It can be seen both from North Deeside Road, on which it stands, and from South Deeside Road, far across the river.

As the work at Marischal College was being competed, His Majesty's Theatre was under construction, designed to be large enough to accommodate high-class performances of all genres, a promise that it has fulfilled ever since.

THE TIVOLI, GUILD STREET 1880 SA000027 (Detail)
(Courtesy of St Andrews University Library)

Here we see Aberdeen's other theatre, the Tivoli. 'I belang tae Glesca', Glasgow's anthem, was written to be performed in this place. Aberdeen's anthem, 'The northern lights of old Aberdeen', was also written in the city, by an Englishwoman married to a Canadian!

Education, Salvation and Damnation

The theatre was built on a very prominent site, visible across the gardens from Union Bridge in the very centre of the city. This site is occupied by just three buildings, all of some importance: the central library, the South Free Kirk (now called St Mark's) and the theatre, all splendid and characteristically Aberdonian in their granite esslar. They are known as Education, Salvation and Damnation. The bureaucracy in Edinburgh does not appreciate the significance of this display of public pride and affection. Damnation is given a category A, as a listed building, Salvation is category B and Education is only given a lowly category C(s). Some would suggest that this speaks volumes about the bureaucrats, while saying little about the buildings.

Union Bridge had been built at only half the width of the street. This must have seemed entirely adequate in 1805, but by 1905, the constriction was proving to be a problem. Arches in steel with the same profile as the original were erected on both sides to carry the pavements, allowing the full width of the granite arch to be occupied by the carriageway. The bridge was still narrower than the street, but now only by a couple of yards. In more recent times, the south arch has been removed and huge steel beams raised to carry a row of shops across that side of the bridge.

The original granite span is still the main structure at the centre of Aberdeen's main street, but it is now difficult to see it, even when one goes down into the gloom of Denburn Road. The widening of the bridge in 1906 involved the removal of the parapets, with their granite balustrades, and their replacement by metal panels with leopards, the city's heraldic beasts, as finials. They were thought by many at the time to be a poor substitute, but are now generally regarded with some affection as 'Kelly's Cats'. William Kelly was the architect of the work. Their removal from the south side was much regretted. Some of them can now be seen in Duthie Park.

There were developments, also, at King's College. 'New King's' was built in 1912, not far from the original and in freestone to match it. Its large classrooms were to prove a great asset when, forty or fifty years later, the numbers of students increased sharply.

THE GRANITE BALUSTRADE ON UNION BRIDGE 1878
SA000005 (Detail)
(Courtesy of University of St Andrews Library)

The old polished granite balustrade along Union Bridge is seen here. Only the short curved endings on the north side now remain as a reminder of the original style.

CASTLE STREET AND THE RAG FAIR c1900 SA000028 (Courtesy of University of St Andrews Library)

The Castlegate is seen here early in the 20th century, still in its traditional role as the marketplace of Aberdeen, with open stalls around the Market Cross. Trams to the beach occupied the north side from 1901 and trams were to take over the whole street in 1936, after which what was left of the market was confined to a nearby site left open by slum clearance. Recent attempts to revive the practice of holding markets in the open have not been particularly successful, except for the 'Timmer Mercat' (Timber Market) in August, a tradition that has survived remarkably well.

The Great North of Scotland Railway rebuilt the joint station shared with the Caledonian Railway, which, together with the North British, ran the trains to and from the south. There were four platforms for lines running right through the station, and nine terminal platforms. The central part of the building was, eccentrically, done in freestone, but the entrance is in granite. Completed in 1913, this was to be the last major work of the Aberdeen-based company.

Then came the First World War! Thousands of men marched off, some in enthusiastic patriotism, some reluctantly. A number refused to go, even suffering imprisonment for their beliefs. Many did not return. Some of those who did come back, even those who were still fit, found that jobs were scarce. They found a nation quite changed from a few years before. In the constrained financial circumstances that applied after the war, the additional expense of cutting granite became a problem for the first time in a century. There would be no more tenements and few villas built in solid grandeur.

After the privations of the war, more attention was given to the housing conditions in which many people had to live. A start was made on the council housing schemes, as they are properly called in Scotland. (Housing estates are an English phenomenon.) Some houses were designed in the style of the tenements, although much more spacious inside. Others consisted of short terraces or, less frequently, semi-detached pairs. They each had a kitchenette and, most importantly, a bathroom with an inside toilet.

Council houses were not for the poorest

A BUNGALOW 2005 A90717k (Norman Miller)

This shows a typical inter-war era bungalow, where granite is used sparingly. This one is on King Street, just in front of a council scheme.

of families. The council wanted to be sure that their tenants would be able to pay the rent. But in their council house, many working-class families had a toilet inside for the first time as well as an adequate number of bedrooms. Significantly, perhaps, some of the largest schemes were at Hilton, just up the hill from Woodside, Seaton and Powis, on either side of Old Aberdeen and in Torry. Private schemes of houses for sale were also built. The cheapest houses were in terraces and were less spacious than most of the council houses, but most were semis or detached. These were popularly called bungalows, although they normally had an upper storey in the roof space.

Most of the new houses, council and private were built in modern, artificial materials.

Brick, little used in Aberdeen for a hundred years, was imported from the large mechanised brickworks in the south. Concrete blocks were made locally. Even where granite was used, the houses had a more slight appearance than those built pre-war. The fashion for large windows may have been welcomed by the householders, but was a real advantage to the builders. Windows are cheaper than walls. Often in the bungalows, the roof would be set immediately above the windows of the ground floor, thus avoiding the need for long granite lintels.

THE BEACH BALLROOM 1938 SA000012 (Detail) (Courtesy of University of St Andrews Library)

Not only houses were built after the war. The council built the Beach Ballroom in remarkably modern style. It was a centre of entertainment for generations of young people in the city, as well as a place to hold conferences and receptions. Its situation beyond the built-up area and next to the sea never seemed to be a problem.

When, in May 1926, the General Council of the Trades Union Congress called a general strike in support of the coal miners, who were facing a cut in their wages, it might have been thought that Aberdeen, ninety miles remote from the nearest coalfield, would be the most reluctant of all major industrial centres. But the diversity of employment and a high regard for education stimulated a radical tradition in the city. The strike was supported enthusiastically. Aberdeen was one of very few places where the main roads were picketed and vehicles without trades union authority turned back. Attempts, admittedly rather half-hearted ones, to have students and other middle-class persons driving trams and buses merely resulted in the scabs being pulled off by strikers, who then drove the vehicles back to the depot. Nan Taylor, who, as a young woman not long out of school, was active in the strike, recalled that some of the older workers may have been worried about the possible use of the army to confront the strikers, but that the young ones were determined, and afraid of nothing.

When the General Council surrendered after only nine days, the strikers in Aberdeen, as elsewhere, had no option but to return to work, if their jobs were still open to them. It was a heavy blow to the resources and the morale of

UNION TERRACE AND GARDENS c1915 A90308

King Edward now presides over the corner occupied since the 1860s by his father. The tall building in the middle ground is the Caledonian Hotel. No trams are in view. Could they have been on strike?

the unions. The Trades Council, shortly after the strike, lost their rather grand headquarters and had to retreat to more modest buildings. In an attempt to reinvigorate the movement, the Scottish TUC called on the Trades Councils to set up Trades Union Organising Committees to extend membership into industries where it was low or even non-existent. Aberdeen Trades Council, on whose initiative the STUC had been organised in the 1890s, was one of only a few which did enough to achieve this aim. The paper mills, on the periphery of the city and employing a large proportion of workers from the more conservative country areas, were the main target. Some success was achieved here and, especially in the post-war period, the unions were strong in many of the paper mills.

Shops and cinemas were also targets for trades union membership, again with some success. But when one of the national leaders of the theatre and cinema workers' union came to address a meeting in Aberdeen, he said that one of the problems with the bosses was that many of them were Jews. George Miller, chairing the meeting on behalf of the Trades Council, immediately made it clear that they were not interested in the bosses' race or religion, but only in how they treated their employees. Sometimes allies can be more obstructive than opponents.

After the First World War, the city lost her place as the major fishing port. Shipyards in Hull and Grimsby were building trawlers bigger than Aberdeen's, and they went further out to sea. The Aberdeen trawlers often went to the Faroes, but the English ones went all the

The Fascists in Aberdeen

Ironically, for a place famed for its left-wing activities, Aberdeen was the only part of Scotland in which the fascists established a noticeable presence. This was due mainly to the determination of a laird (country landlord) named William Keith Abercrombie Jopp Chambers-Hunter. He joined the British Union of Fascists in 1936 and tirelessly campaigned for them, but was opposed by well-organised left-wingers, who had the considerable ranks of the unemployed as their eyes and ears. The fascists tried their standard procedures of meetings and marches, but both were consistently disrupted. In any case, the fascists had essentially been defeated in London by the time they got started in Aberdeen. The local leaders resigned in March 1939.

way to Iceland and even to the Grand Banks off Newfoundland. The shorter distance from the Humber to the big English cities also counted in their favour. In conditions of recession, there was little money available for renewing the fleet. Many of the trawlers that did put to sea worked at a loss. One new development was the production of cod liver oil. Trawlers carried a steel vessel, the liver jar, into which the livers were dropped as the fish were brought aboard. One local firm, Isaac Spenser and Co, whose main business was the manufacture of paint, had a small boat, called 'Isco', which went round the trawlers in the Albert Basin collecting the contents of the liver jars.

THE FREE SOUTH CHURCH AND PUBLIC LIBRARY 1892 SA000020 (Courtesy of University of St Andrews Library)

This shows the view before the erection of His Majesty's Theatre. The building that can be seen in the background is the Royal Infirmary, designed by Archibald Simpson in 1832 and standing on Woolmanhill. Under the dome was the operating theatre, which really was a theatre. Students sat all round learning the trade at a time before anaesthetics had been discovered! Greatly extended in 1896, this was the north-east's main hospital until the opening of Forresterhill in 1936. It is now used largely as a store for medical equipment.

SMOKING HADDIES 1902 SA000038 (Courtesy of University of St Andrews Library)

Fish were prepared in various ways for the consumer. They could be packed in salt, frozen, canned or, as here, smoked. The number of fish that had to be handled is obvious in this picture. This is the Scottish fishery at its high point.

Worried about the effects on society of large numbers of unemployed men, the government started schemes to provide work. At the same time, the growing numbers of motor vehicles were crowding the roads. Getting the unemployed to build new roads seemed to go some way towards solving both problems. So a road was driven through from Kittybrewster, just south of Woodside to King Street. This passed right through Old Aberdeen. Houses immediately behind the Town House were demolished to make way for the new road, called St Machar Drive, which was slightly narrower here than in the rest of its length. This was achieved with remarkably little impact on the integrity of the old burgh. The Town House remained complete and substantial granite walls were built around the gaps.

The independent hospitals had long planned to move out of the city centre, now heavily polluted, to a green site at Forresterhill. As there was no agreement about the details, the Sick Children's Hospital moved on its own in 1926. Aware that medical ideas were changing rapidly, the trustees decided to build a temporary structure. This would be cheaper, and could be easily dismantled when something more modern was thought necessary. It was finally demolished on the completion of the new building in 2004! The Maternity Hospital followed a few years later, but the Royal Infirmary was slow in gathering enough funds to build a new place. Lord Provost Andrew Lewis, who had started a shipyard in Torry in 1916, took the lead. He raised substantial donations from some wealthy friends, such as the Earl and Countess Cowdray. There followed a huge fund-raising campaign, to which virtually the whole population contributed.

Many local organisations made great efforts to raise funds for the new hospital, among them the co-operative guilds, which were vigorously active throughout the city and its periphery. HRH the Duke of York, who was shortly to become King George VI, came officially to open the Infirmary in 1936.

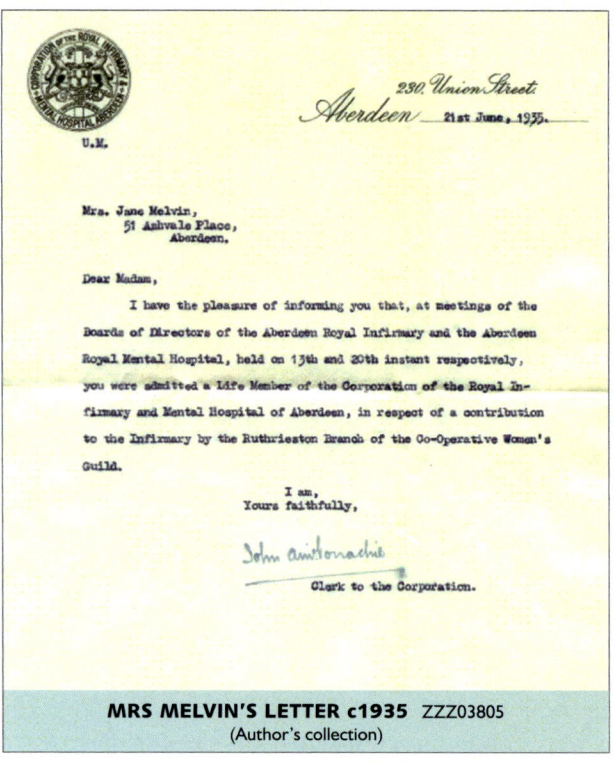

MRS MELVIN'S LETTER c1935 ZZZ03805
(Author's collection)

A letter to Mrs Jane Melvin (the author's grandmother), thanking her for her contribution to the fundraising for the Royal Infirmary and Mental Hospital of Aberdeen.

Scandal in the Royal Family

While his younger brother was opening the hospital, King Edward VIII was seen at the Joint Station, awaiting Mrs Simpson. One of those who saw him was a reporter with the local papers, but, of course, nothing was said officially at the time. It seems, however, that most of the population of Aberdeen knew what was happening, and despite the blackout in the press, few were surprised that the abdication crisis followed shortly afterwards.

The royal family were not alone in taking their holidays in the north-east. Trains brought thousands of summer visitors, making Aberdeen the largest holiday resort in Scotland. No one at this time expected a week of sunshine on holiday. It was enough to have fresh air. Aberdeen's size and the long beach and links, the grassy area just back from the sand, ensured that that was in plentiful supply, as the breezes off the sea kept these places clear.

Most of the holiday-makers came from Glasgow during the 'Fair', when the city more or less shut down for a week. In Aberdeen, its equivalent was called the Trades Week. Shipbuilding, engineering and the building trades stopped work. Many of the mills stopped production, providing an opportunity for the maintenance staff to repair and renew the machines.

Council staff at the Town House also went on holiday during the Trades Week. One year, they returned to find that the coal fires in the rooms had been replaced with electric heaters. This was not welcomed by the water department staff. They had developed ways of bringing in extra coal when the town sergeant was not looking and always had the warmest offices in the building.

In 1939, the Established Kirk built St Mary's on King Street to serve the new schemes on the east side of the street. A modest building, as befits its purpose and its times, this was to be the last completely granite building in the Granite City. It is an active kirk still.

As the storm clouds gathered over Europe, more jobs were created. Hall, Russell and Co, which had been idle, started building ships again and other firms increased their activity.

Then came the Second World War. Again men marched away to war. Many in the local regiment, the Gordon Highlanders, were trapped in France, along with the bulk of the Scottish contingent. They were to spend five years as prisoners of war. But this time it was not only the soldiers who found themselves in the firing line.

Aberdeen had more air raid alerts than anywhere else in Scotland. In the direct line from northern Germany to the great industrial complexes of Clydeside, Aberdeen was frequently a target of the Luftwaffe. In total, 250 civilians were killed and many

During the Second World War, Britain and Germany both worked on radar to detect enemy aeroplanes as they came in to attack. Both also tried to confuse the other's systems. To do this effectively, it was necessary to have an example of the other side's equipment, to see how it worked.

On the ninth of May, 1943, Herbert Schmidt took off from Denmark to fly to Norway, both occupied by the Nazis at this time, in a Ju88, with the secret Liechtenstein equipment aboard. But he turned westwards and, when challenged by an American fighter from Dyce, Schmidt lowered his landing gear, the equivalent, for an aeroplane, of showing a white flag. The German bomber was escorted into Dyce, where the Liechtenstein was recovered undamaged.

Many details of this episode have not been made public. This includes the eventual fate of Herbert Schmidt.

THE BEACH AND THE BATHING STATION c1910 A90319

Although taken about 1910, this scene would be familiar to visitors in the Twenties and Thirties. There was no need to take off any clothes, just because folk were on a beach! It seems not to have been a sunny day. That would not matter. Visitors came for the fresh air.

Did you know?

Asked to raise enough money to pay for a new warship, the people of Aberdeen honoured their commitment faster than the authorities could cope! £2,750,000 was what was required (£57,000,000 in todays values). Before the fund could be closed, well over £3,000,000 had been subscribed.

buildings destroyed. Many of those who lived through the war still speak of a full or nearly full moon on a clear night as a 'bombers' moon'. In such conditions, even with the black-out, the pilots could see the moonlight shimmering on the two rivers and they knew that there was a city with shipyards and other industries, just below them. At the end of this war, there had been more destruction, but less loss of life. More importantly, the popular mood was completely different. People were, in general, optimistic and determined to make things better.

Housing was in great demand. Nothing could be built during the war and many houses had been destroyed. There were also factories that had been producing materials for the forces, and which were now at a standstill. Two problems were solved by turning these factories over to manufacturing prefabricated houses. Constructed inside, where bad weather caused no delays, they were taken, each in four sections, to be lifted on to brick foundations and fastened together. Never had houses been built so quickly. Designed to be temporary until permanent houses could be

provided, there are, sadly, none of them left in Aberdeen. Virtually everyone who lived in the prefabs remembers them with great affection.

More conventional housing was also started immediately after the war. Like the prefabs, the schemes were mostly just on the edge of the built-up area, gradually extending the city. Most were in brick or concrete blocks on the pre-war patterns.

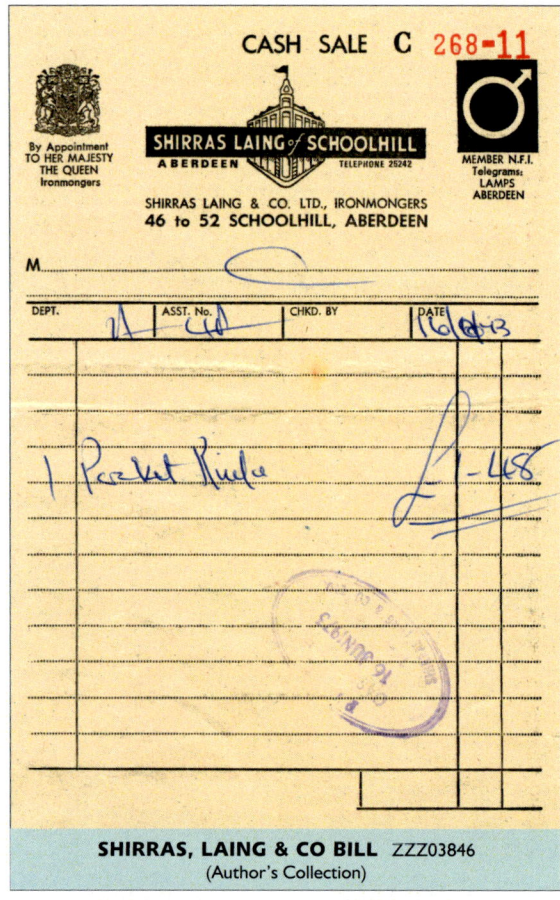

SHIRRAS, LAING & CO BILL ZZZ03846
(Author's Collection)

Before the days of the supermarket, many shops were locally owned. Shirras, Laing & Co supplied good quality kitchenware, electrical goods and gardening equipment. Like many others, it is sadly missed.

One of the planned changes carried out in the 1930s was the laying-out of a road to bypass the old Brig o' Dee. Beautiful and historic, the old bridge could not cope with the volumes of traffic that had by then built up. The new road led to a new bridge downstream of the old. In an interesting compromise, the bridge was a concrete structure faced in granite, with granite cutwaters doing the job at which granite excelled. Work was not complete when war broke out, but continued till the project was finished. King George VI came in 1941 to open the bridge, which is named after him.

The new bridge opened up the possibility of building houses on the south bank of the river, with direct access to the city. Indeed plans to do this had been made before the war. The area, called Kincorth, had been incorporated into the city when its boundaries were again extended in 1937. As soon as hostilities ceased, work began. Here the houses were built with some granite, although all the pillars, sills and lintels were in synthetic granite. Still, the scheme looked very grand and traditional at a glance. This was to be the last large-scale use of the local stone.

Some houses were built partly with granite, usually in areas in the central parts of the city, where they were replacing old buildings. These were mostly council houses, but included a few private dwellings. The great quarry at Rubislaw closed in 1972. The last of the granite from Rubislaw was used in a small scheme of council houses on Spital, part of the old ridgeway from the royal burgh to Old Aberdeen. Europe's largest man-made hole was allowed to fill slowly with water.

GRANITE AND CROCUSES IN KINCORTH 2005 A90724k (Norman Miller)

Council housing schemes are seldom regarded as tourist attractions. The older, granite parts of Kincorth, 'The Queen o The Schemes', could be an exception.

ALBERT BASIN 1902 SA000039 (Detail)
(Courtesy of University of St Andrews Library)

At her berth in the Albert Basin, the cylindrical funnel shows this vessel to be a steamship, while the otter board lashed to the gallows at the stern shows that she is a trawler. Steam was still dominant after the war, but soon diesels were to take over.

There was plenty of work after 1945. Exhausted and impoverished by the war, Britain needed to grow or catch as much of her own food as she could, and to manufacture articles for export. The fishing fleet was busy. So were the fish houses curing and packing the catch, and so were all the suppliers to the boats. Aberdeen stuck to the smaller middle distance trawlers, leaving the English ports to specialise in the longer trips, as had been the case before the war. The shipyards had many fishing boats and other vessels to build, making up for wartime losses and pre-war under-investment. Engineering works, paper and textile mills and the chemical works were

all in demand. For some time, the old order seemed to be reasserting itself, but with better pay and conditions for the workers. But from the 1950s big changes were being planned.

The corporation had started to use buses after the First World War and two of the tram routes had been abandoned in 1931, although some of those which remained were extended, the last as late as 1938. But

Aberdeen's Foremost Fashion Shop

We cordially invite you to make WATT & GRANT your Store while in Aberdeen.
You may walk through our Fashion Salons at your leisure. Accessories and Linens are on the ground floor and you will find many lovely things in the Gift Salon, lower ground floor (downstairs from the Book Shop).
Meet your friends in the Restaurant (Third Floor— elevator direct). It is noted for its excellent service and good food, supervised by our Chef de Cuisine.

Watt & Grant
"WHERE QUALITY COUNTS"

221 UNION ST., ABERDEEN

WATT AND GRANT ADVERTISEMENT ZZZ03850
(Author's Collection)

This was one of the city's more exclusive shops, situated in the western half of Union Street. The impressive granite building remains, but the shop was bought, along with many of the local independents, by the House of Fraser. It did not long survive.

now abandonment of the whole system was planned. The routes closed one by one. The last, the trunk route of four and a half miles all the way across the city from the Bridge of Dee to the Bridge of Don, being abandoned in May 1958.

The end of the tramway showed, in sharp contrast, the difference between popular and official attitudes to the life of the city.

On their final day, 70,000 people turned out to see the trams running for the last time. Even allowing for quite large numbers of enthusiasts coming from outside the north-east, this must mean that something like one-third of the population came to bid farewell to this most fondly regarded system of transport.

UNION STREET c1900 A90309

Trams add to the elegance of the great street in a way no other vehicle can. From 1900 to 1958, electric trams were useful and graceful along the length of Union Street. Immediately in front of the tower of the Town House, the dome and the whole building below it have been demolished, as has the building in the right extreme foreground. Every other building in this picture survives to this day.

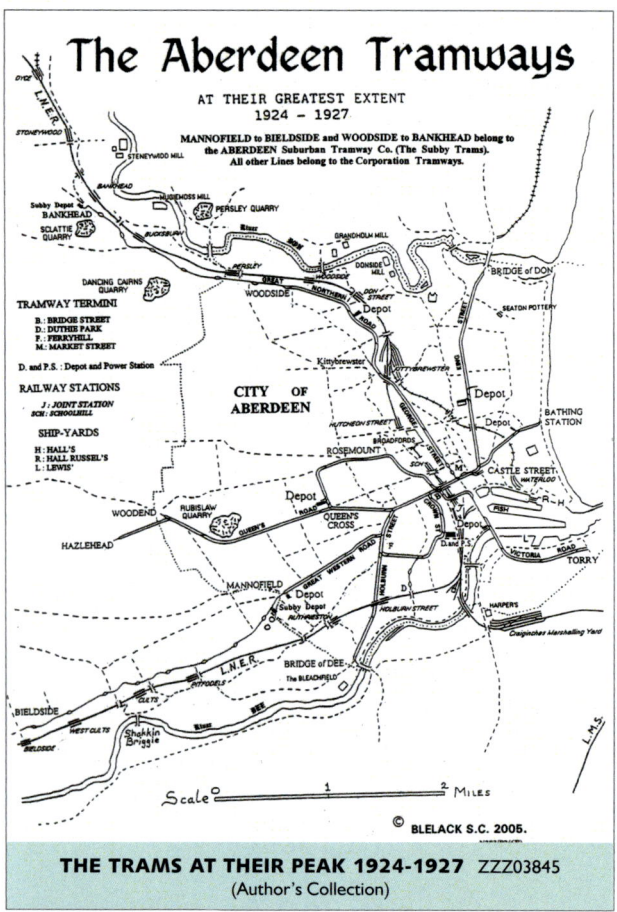

THE TRAMS AT THEIR PEAK 1924-1927 ZZZ03845
(Author's Collection)

The corporation ran nine routes, some right to the city boundaries. Shown also is the route of the subby trains, with its many stations close together.

The corporation sent their oldest tram to Edinburgh, no doubt confident that she would be consigned to the basement of the Royal Museum of Scotland and never seen again. The rest of the fleet, including twenty large streamlined trams only nine years old, was burned for scrap. The mindless modernisers were in charge of public affairs in the city. They had no interest in preserving any of its history, except in documents. It is hard now to find any evidence that we ever had trams.

Fortunately, something went wrong with the plans and a transport museum was opened at Alford, thirty miles west of Aberdeen, where Tram No 1 can now be seen, along with much else of interest.

The End of an Era

Only eight years after the last of the trams, another sad loss in the field of transport occurred when British Railways withdrew the last of the steam engines. But there was a grand flourish in the last years. Several 'Streaks', the streamlined A4 Pacifics, the fastest steam locomotives in the world, worked the passenger trains between Aberdeen and Glasgow. One of them, 'Union of South Africa' is preserved privately and can sometimes be seen hauling enthusiasts' specials.

Slum clearance was originally just that. But as the worst of the old properties were demolished, it increasingly became a way of reshaping the city. Sound buildings, which could have continued in use, were demolished because they did not fit into the plans. Whole sections of the city centre were cleared of nearly all their old buildings and with these went most of the last remnants of the medieval street plan which had survived the Georgian rebuilding.

In the ancient street called Netherkirkgate (the low way to the kirk) stood Benholm's

Lodging, a country laird's town house, built about 1610. It would have been swept away with everything else in this historic street had not Lord Marks, the descendant of one of the founders of Marks and Spencer, made a substantial donation towards its transfer. The site was about to be occupied by a much extended rebuilding of the shop, known in Aberdeen as 'Markie's'.

Benholm's Lodging was the only Z-plan house in a Scottish burgh. So what did the council do with the money? They put the house out to Tillydrone, a place which, while inside the city boundary, has all the appearance of being rural. Perched atop the steep bank of the River Don about a quarter of a mile up from St Machar's Cathedral, the old house looks just like a baronial castle in remote countryside. It was for some time quite the grandest council house in Britain. The first tenant was Dr William Douglas Simpson, the university librarian and Scotland's foremost authority on the history of ancient buildings.

PROVOST SKENE'S HOUSE 2005 A90705k (Norman Miller)

Dating from 1545 this is the only survivor of this part of the old city centre. It is surrounded by St Nicholas House, which people in Aberdeen have just voted the place they would most like to see demolished.

The whole historic area between the Netherkirkgate and the Upperkirkgate was cleared, except for Provost Skene's House, which was only saved by the intervention of HM the Queen Mother, while on an official visit to the City. Let it not be said that there are no advantages to being a royal burgh!

The house has led an interesting life. The painted gallery, of about 1625, is a rare but unfortunately no longer complete example of Protestant devotional art. Provost Sir George Skene modernised much of it from 1669 onwards. The house had the misfortune to be occupied by 'Butcher' Cumberland in the winter of 1746. Later, it became the Victoria Lodging House. Since its restoration in the 1950s, it has been a museum of urban life. It is now surrounded by the huge and utterly styleless St Nicholas House, where many of the council headquarters staff work. Thankfully, there are now plans to demolish this blot on the landscape.

A house associated with another provost has also survived in another ancient street. Shiprow was the principal route from the Castlegate to the harbour before the building of Marischal Street. Dating from 1594, the house was occupied in the early 18th century by Provost John Ross of Arnage. This, with an adjacent house, of about 1750 and the former Trinity Congregational Kirk of 1877, is now incorporated in the Maritime Museum. These are the only two remaining domestic buildings in the royal burgh that date from before the

PROVOST ROSS'S HOUSE 2005 A90707k (Norman Miller)

This is now part of the Maritime Museum. The provost would have wanted to be close to his work at the quayside.

middle of the 18th century, a fact which shows the extent to which the city has been reconstructed over the past two hundred and fifty years. Old Aberdeen, despite its much smaller size overall, has several houses of this period. These include a cottage on Grant's Place with the date 1732 over the door.

In the trendy sixties, social attitudes and beliefs were changing. Men let their hair and beards grow to an extent that had not been acceptable for half a century. Clothes became more colourful. But these were only the visible tips of an iceberg of changes at every level. The radical traditions of the city continued to be seen in the large and vibrant membership of the youth wing of the Ban the Bomb movement, which continued throughout most of the sixties, while the national movement was faltering.

Holidays were changing. Aberdeen still received the crowds from Glasgow during the Fair, now two weeks long. But increasing numbers were choosing to fly to Spain on charter flights. Tourism was becoming less important here as the decade proceeded, and it would continue to decline.

THE DREADED TYPHOID ZZZ03847 (Author's Collection)

In 1964 Aberdeen suffered an outbreak of typhoid, which infected 504 people. It started with infected meat from a can of corned beef from Argentina. A great campaign to be especially clean was launched, of which this leaflet was a part. The council instituted the annual Festival of Bon Accord to celebrate the end of the outbreak. We later leant that the government knew about the unhygienic conditions in the canned meat industry in Argentina, but did nothing, because they did not want to damage trade.

THE BEACH BATHS 1878 SA000026 (Detail)
(Courtesy of University of St Andrews Library)

The Beach Baths were where many Aberdonians learnt to swim. Unusually built in brick, but thus matching the nearby retort houses of the gas works, the Baths used sea water, heated a little. Nothing of this much-loved place now exists. The site is occupied by a small mound of grass, and it is hard to believe that there ever was a building there.

The New Urban Myth about Union Street

In 1964 the town council decided that there should be Christmas lights in Union Street. They sent a delegation to London to discuss buying the lights hung in Regent Street the year before. During a tea break, one of the London lighting men asked if Aberdeen had a street that could take the lights from the metropolis's main street. The Aberdeen lighting men were able to tell them that Union Street is as wide as Regent Street, it is longer than Regent Street, and it is older than Regent Street. The lights from London did appear in Union Street, that year, which has had Christmas lights made up by the Aberdeen lighting department every year since.

Industrial work continued much as it had. Grandholm wove the Crombie cloth, which became very fashionable. Broadford Mill, long established near the city centre, made the hoses for the London fire brigade. Pirie Appleton's made the headed stationery for 10 Downing Street, used by several Prime Ministers.

Diesel engines replaced steam on the ships. Lewis's shipyard manufactured a Doxford engine, a very sophisticated diesel, under license. The idea was to make a smaller version of the Doxford, suitable for the Aberdeen trawler. It was said that a Doxford, which was for a diesel unusually free of vibration, could safely be run while merely standing in the machine shop, whereas any other diesel would certainly have to be bolted to the floor. There was not a happy ending to this brave attempt at harnessing the new technology. Mechanically the engine was a success, but it was too expensive. The shipyard bought engines from the south after this experiment. It was an indication of the extent of the problems that were soon to come. Still, the yard built the first factory trawler, 'Fairtry' and the topsail schooner 'Malcolm Miller' for the Sail Training Association.

The industries that had been so important and so successful for Aberdeen for two centuries faced increasing competition both from larger firms in the south of Britain, with the advantage of economies of scale and from industries abroad, with much lower labour costs. Despite the continued high quality of their products and some efforts at modernisation, the local firms were beginning to lose their markets. New styles of fishing were being developed, but the skippers engaged in these felt that the fish market at Aberdeen gave a privileged position to the trawlers. The new boats turned increasingly to Peterhead and Fraserburgh on the north-east corner of Scotland. These both had large harbours extended for the herring fishery in the 19th century. They were delighted to have the chance to see these harbours fully used.

But Aberdeen was seeing something new and, for the great majority of us, completely unexpected. Strange vessels started to appear in the harbour in the 1960s. Some seemed to have huge pylons amidships, like those carrying the National Grid electric cables. They were drilling for oil in the North Sea, from structures called rigs, most of which were too big to enter the harbour here.

In 1971 the large Forties Field was proved. Now the oil started to flow ashore. Scotland found herself in the company of Persia and Saudi Arabia as a producer of the most valuable commodity in the world's economy. Gigantic structures called platforms were built to tap the new resource. They were miles out to sea and could not be seen from the coast.

SHELL EXPLORATION HEADQUARTERS 2005 A90708k (Norman Miller)

Shell's exploration of the North Sea is controlled from here, one of very few late 20th century buildings that are worth a second glance. The gold-tinted windows glow in certain light conditions.

But the platforms had to be supplied with drilling equipment, machinery to do their work, pipes to carry the oil and food and domestic supplies for the men who worked aboard for a fortnight at a time. An odd style of vessel, with a high superstructure for'ard and the rest of her length occupied by a flat platform became a common sight in the harbour. These were the supply boats which ferried the equipment to the platforms.

Like the trawlers, the supply boats are gregarious. A few came to Aberdeen first and the others all followed. Many other ports made great efforts to attract them, but with little success.

The platforms also needed men to be taken to them. This was done by helicopter, the only vehicle that could get there quickly and land on the limited space available.

Aberdeen's airport at Dyce, six miles from the city centre, became the busiest heliport in the world.

Aberdeen men found work on the oil-rigs and platforms. But many more were needed. This led to a substantial flow of people into the city. Aberdeen had not seen anything like

THE ROUNDHOUSE AND A SUPPLY BOAT 2005 A90712k (Norman Miller)

A supply boat returns past the Roundhouse (which is actually octagonal). From here, the Harbour Board records all vessels entering and leaving the port.

this before. The great increase of population in the 19th century had come about by natural increase or immigration largely from the rural north-east. The city had no real influx of Irish, Jews or Italians, although small numbers did arrive before the First World War. Nor had there been West Indians after the Second World War and only a few Indians came to open restaurants, which quickly became as popular as they were in other parts of Britain. The largest numbers of oil workers came from the south-west of Scotland and the north-east of England. But we had also a different kind of immigrant. Executives and managers came from France, the Netherlands and the USA.

Some local firms did well by making or maintaining things for the oil industry and many new companies sprang up to do this. There were an even greater number which supplied the oil industry with both equipment and men. Even the academic institutions were involved. The geology and economics departments of the university were in demand and Gordon's Institute of Technology took responsibility for providing safety courses. Soon, only those who had the certificates from these would be employed on the rigs and platforms.

THE SOUTH BREAKWATER 1935 SA000011 (Courtesy of University of St Andrews Library)

The power of the sea is as much of a threat to oil supply boats as to trawlers and coasters. The South Breakwater, seen here, and the longer and older North Breakwater protect the harbour and all vessels therein.

Pluses and Minuses of Black Gold

The arrival of the oil industry protected Aberdeen from the steep rise in unemployment that was general throughout the country at this time. But there was a price to pay, in a very literal sense. The prices of everything - food, clothes and other commodities - increased enormously. This was especially true of house prices, and Aberdeen became the third most expensive place in Britain, after London and Brighton. This made for real problems because the city certainly did not have the third highest wages in the country. For most people living in Aberdeen the coming of oil was, to say the least of it, a mixed blessing. The presence of the oil industry, with its huge resources, hastened the decline of the traditional industries of the city. Companies closed and no great attempt was made to reverse this tendency. The loss of much of the fish landings was accepted because the Harbour Board was interested only in the oil. The political authorities, local and national, dazzled by the new arrival, did little to counteract the decline.

The power of the oil industry was demonstrated by the fate of Old Torry, a fishing village that had existed for centuries. Many of its traditional houses were over a hundred years old. The council had started to arrange for this place to be designated a conservation area, which would have given it a degree of protection. The oil firms wanted the site for a tank farm. The council immediately surrendered. The whole village was demolished.

**STUDENTS' CHARITIES DIAMOND JUBILEE
T-SHIRT** ZZZ03841 (Paul Baron)

Students used to dress in fancy costume and collect money among the Saturday shoppers, and thousands turned out to see a parade of floats in the evening. Students in Aberdeen regularly collected almost as much as their counterparts in Glasgow, a city five times the size and much wealthier.

What the local council was obsessed with was the Comprehensive Development Area, although 'Comprehensive Destruction Area' would have been a more accurate title. A considerable section of the city centre, consisting largely of our unique granite buildings in sound condition, was swept away to make way for closed shopping centres, of absolutely no architectural interest and containing all the same shops as can be found in any other city.

Many of the shops in the area came together to oppose the development. 'Don't break the heart of the Granite City!' was their slogan. They produced alternative plans, retaining the streets and most of the traditional buildings. They were completely ignored.

If modern planning had a bad effect on the city centre, it was a disaster for Woodside. The main street there, Great Northern Road, is part of the main road from Aberdeen to Inverness. To make the section through Woodside a dual carriageway, most of the buildings on both sides were demolished. The wide road of today is now more congested than the narrower one of yesterday. Woodside had been destroyed as a community for no advantage to anyone else. It must be hard for those who cannot remember what Woodside used to be to imagine that it ever was a cohesive community, indeed a burgh. There used to be every kind of shop on Great Northern and people wanted to go there. Now people want only to avoid it. It used to be a main street. Now it is only a main road.

Partly in response to such developments,

GEORGE STREET TRADERS ACTION GROUP
ZZZ03848 (Author's Collection)

Leaflets and adverts with this well-designed slogan and symbol were widely distributed. Many now regret that their ideas did not carry the day.

Did you know?

Aberdeen is the champion city in Europe for the finding of coin hoards. Hoards consist of large numbers of coins deliberately buried, perhaps at times of threat to the owners or the city, or before the owner went on a journey. Whatever the reason, the owner did not return to recover his treasure. Most of the coins are sterling. Some are Scottish. One hoard, still in what is left of the pot in which it was buried, is displayed at the entrance to one of the new shopping centres. Single coins are rarely found in archaeological digs in Aberdeen!

a new style of community action arose, here as in other cities. One result of this was 'Aberdeen People's Press', which published a fortnightly paper highlighting the problems and opportunities of these changes.

Old Aberdeen survived essentially intact. From the 1950s to the 1970s, the numbers of students at the university rose sharply. New buildings were required for classrooms, laboratories, administrative offices and other purposes. The university eventually bought nearly all the houses anywhere near King's College. The chemistry building, of the mid-1950s, was an unusual cruciform shape and used quite a lot of granite very badly. The slightly later natural philosophy building used a little granite rather well. At its centre is a wide dome, which, while made of anonymous concrete, is a pleasing and unusual shape. Both are situated just to the west of the High Street, out of sight while one is walking there, but very easy of access to the students and staff. Nearby is the contemporary Crombie Hall, Aberdeen's first hall of residence, an oddity in concrete and wood. After this, the university put up buildings of no merit, except that most of them were fairly low. But two of the new multi-storey structures, the agriculture building at the eastern and the zoology building at the western edges of the university's territory, compete with each other to be the ugliest and most offensive. Agriculture wins, if only because, placed near King Street, it is the more readily noticed.

In 1975 there was a major reorganisation of local government throughout Scotland. A tradition lasting eight centuries was swept aside with the abolition of the burghs, leaving only the four counties of cities. Even these were reduced to being districts, with limited powers, submerged in Regions, which controlled most of the functions of local government. After all this, the leaders in various fields of our national life sometimes wonder why a younger generation does not respect the traditions of our country!

Aberdeen's boundaries were again extended. Unlike 1937, but like 1891, the city now incorporated long-established built-up areas. The rather posh Cults and the paper-mill town of Culter on Deeside were included. So were Bucksburn and Bankhead, including the paper mills of Mugiemoss and Stoneywood, Dyce, with its airport and Lawson's bacon and pie works, to the south

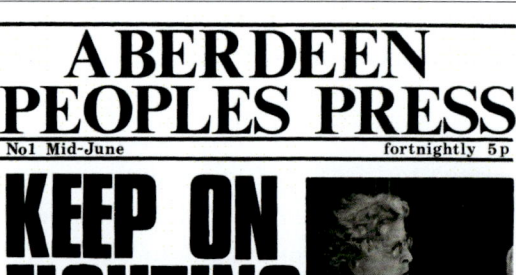

THE 'PEOPLE'S PRESS' ZZZ03854
(Author's Collection)

Published for several years by a small group of enthusiasts, this paper acted as a focus for the new style of community activism.

of the Don. Also included was Cove, to the south of Torry and, like it, containing an old fishing village. But the largest population was in the suburb of Bridge of Don.

The Bridge of Don started as a small group of houses on the north side of the bridge. Small schemes of council and private houses had been built before and after the Second World War. Many young couples, unable to find houses in Aberdeen, moved there, and with the influx of new people looking for work in the oil industry, this growth increased.

"Taste that
Finer Flavour"
in
SAUSAGES
BACON
and
PORK
from

LAWSON OF **DYCE**

FRESH
from the
FACTORY
in the Country

to your Northern Co-operative Shop

THE FACTORY IN THE COUNTRY ZZZ03901
(Author's Collection)

Situated at the northern edge of Dyce, Lawson's supplied not only the Co-opie, but many national Firms, including Markie's.

Although industrial estates have been laid out here, most people who live in the Bridge of Don work in the city. Their journeys to and fro over only two bridges fit for modern traffic are made worse by having to compete with commuters coming in from the greatly expanded towns to the north. Despite this, the council has given permission for huge housing developments in the past thirty years, raising the population of the Bridge of Don to about 30,000. The suburb is now bigger than any town north of Aberdeen, except Inverness and may well be Europe's largest suburb. Other parts of the outer areas have also seen large housing developments but none on the scale of the Bridge of Don, despite its geographical position.

Also included in the city was a large tract of open countryside to the west. Aberdeen, with a population in its expanded area of 210,000 could be swallowed up in the Grampian region, total population about 500,000. But Glasgow, with about 750,000 people, could only be included in a huge region. So Strathclyde was created, with nearly half the Scottish population in it. The other half was distributed across eight regions, one of which, Borders, was smaller than many of the districts, including Aberdeen. This irrational and shabby arrangement did not last long.

THE BRIDGE OF DON 1938 SA000010
(Courtesy of University of St Andrews Library)

A salmon fisherman sets out with his nets from Nether Don. In the background is the new Bridge of Don, in 2005 a mere 175 years old. It also has been widened, its width doubled in 1958, by building a concrete bridge of the same size and shape as the granite original. The parapets have been reinstated and new granite used on the new south face. The whole area beyond it, now including a suburb of 30,000 inhabitants, is named after it.

THE SOUTH KIRK AND THE MITHER KIRK c1900
SA000006 (Detail) (Courtesy of University of St Andrews Library)

Social change towards the end of the 20th century is demonstrated by the two towers in this picture. Left: the South Kirk, by John Smith, 1830. This seemed to be his favourite design for kirks, as he produced something very similar for St Clement's, the Kirk of Fittie, and for Nigg parish. None of these is presently functioning as a kirk. Indeed, the South Kirk is now a pub. Right: the tower and spire of the Mither Kirk, as rebuilt, by William Smith, after the medieval wooden spire was burned in 1874. This one still is a kirk.

In 1996 there was yet another fundamental reorganisation. Aberdeen, again along with the other cities, regained her independence, as an all-purpose authority. This time there were no changes to the city boundaries. This is quite remarkable, as the city now includes a large area of open rural land right up to the edge of the large built-up area of Westhill, which has never been anything but a suburb of Aberdeen, but which is outwith the City in political terms.

Aberdeen has always had a large and active voluntary sector. Several organisations are grouped into Voluntary Service Aberdeen, started in 1890 as the Association for Improving the Condition of the Poor. It has seen profound changes in both the needs to be met and basic attitudes in society. The old name simply could not be used today!

Agecare, part of VSA, runs many homes for elderly people and has constantly renewed the buildings and the service provided by their staff. The Children's Society now works mostly with children with special needs. Linn Moor School provides education in a residential setting for some of these children. St Aubin's provides a supportive environment for those recovering from mental health problems. At Easter Anguston, there is an extensive farming and gardening establishment where young adults with learning difficulties work and study new skills. VSA has recently taken over responsibility for the Carers' Centre, which provides support to carers in the community. The Association also run a number of charity shops. This sector provides a high proportion of the small shops that are still in existence, as well as contributing to the funds of their organisers and providing many pleasant days' shopping for the considerable body of enthusiasts of this genre.

The Workers' Educational Association (WEA) has been active in the city since the 1920s. There are at present several classes discussing local history and local affairs in general, mostly attended by retired people. In 1974, the Association, in conjunction with women's liberation groups, started to organise classes which encouraged women to look afresh at their own lives and to consider returning to formal education, if they thought that this was right for them. Many of those who came had never thought that they would be able to go to university, but, with encouragement while in these classes, several of them did and went on to start professional careers.

As a result of the success of the early classes, a programme was drawn up as a guide to future action in this field. Called 'Getting

SEVERE CLASSICAL GRANITE 2005 A90709k (Norman Miller)

This shows some 1830s houses, probably by John Smith, on King Street. This is how restrained the city's buildings were, even in the centre. The WEA now occupies the floors above the shop.

Started', this was to be adopted by the WEA nationally as their standard for such work. In 1988, the WEA in Aberdeen worked with the Department of Employment to provide innovative and individually tailored activities for the long-term unemployed. Called the 'Reach-out Project' and widely praised as a great success in bringing new opportunities and new hope to this group, this continues, with funds from the National Lottery.

Several kinds of adult education now provided by the Colleges started with the WEA. These include trades union education and adult literacy, where the WEA locally proved that there was a real need for such work. The Association is still active in this field today.

Did you know?
BRITAIN IN BLOOM

Aberdeen has won the Britain in Bloom competition more often than any other city. Indeed, so regularly did we win, that we were banned from the competition for a year to give other places a chance. David Welsh, who, as Director of Links and Parks, was in overall charge of the effort, was later made superintendent of the Royal Parks in London. He returned to Aberdeen in retirement. The new winter garden in Duthie Park, a central feature of the council's horticultural efforts and home of their prize-winning collection of cacti, is named after him.

SWAN POND, DUTHIE PARK c1900 A90315

Elizabeth Crombie Duthie (1818-1885) bought this area and gave it to the citizens of Aberdeen as a public park in 1880. It contains two ponds, one used for sailing model boats. The obelisk commemorating Sir James MacGrigor, transferred from the quad at Marischal at the start of the 20th century, can be seen here. A statue of Hygeia, goddess of health, commemorates the donor.

CHAPTER FIVE

Looking Forward

THE 21ST CENTURY STARTED, just as the 20th had done, as a continuation of what went immediately before. There were no startling new developments, as was the case two centuries previously.

The last of Aberdeen's textile mills, Broadfords, closed late in 2004, leaving its workers not only without their jobs, but also without their pensions. The new owners will make a handsome profit from the value of the site, as has happened with several recent closures.

This leaves the city even more dependent on the oil industry. The shipyards have all closed, very little fish is landed and the fish processing industry is, obviously enough, much reduced. Only one firm remains working granite and that is all imported. The engineering that remains is mostly closely tied to oil. Only two paper mills are left, one of which is due to close in June 2005. The diversity of employment, which was such a benefit to generations of Aberdonians, is much restricted.

Oil continues to provide work of a wide variety and Aberdeen is dramatically more prosperous than many other old industrial cities. With that prosperity comes the chance to avoid the worst of the social and health problems which afflict some others.

But oil is a wasting asset and the peak of production in the North Sea is already past. The platforms will continue to produce for decades to come, but the industry will become smaller. Many firms are making efforts to find markets for specialised products and services in the new oil provinces in the South Atlantic and Central Asia. But it will not be the same as having a major province on the city's doorstep.

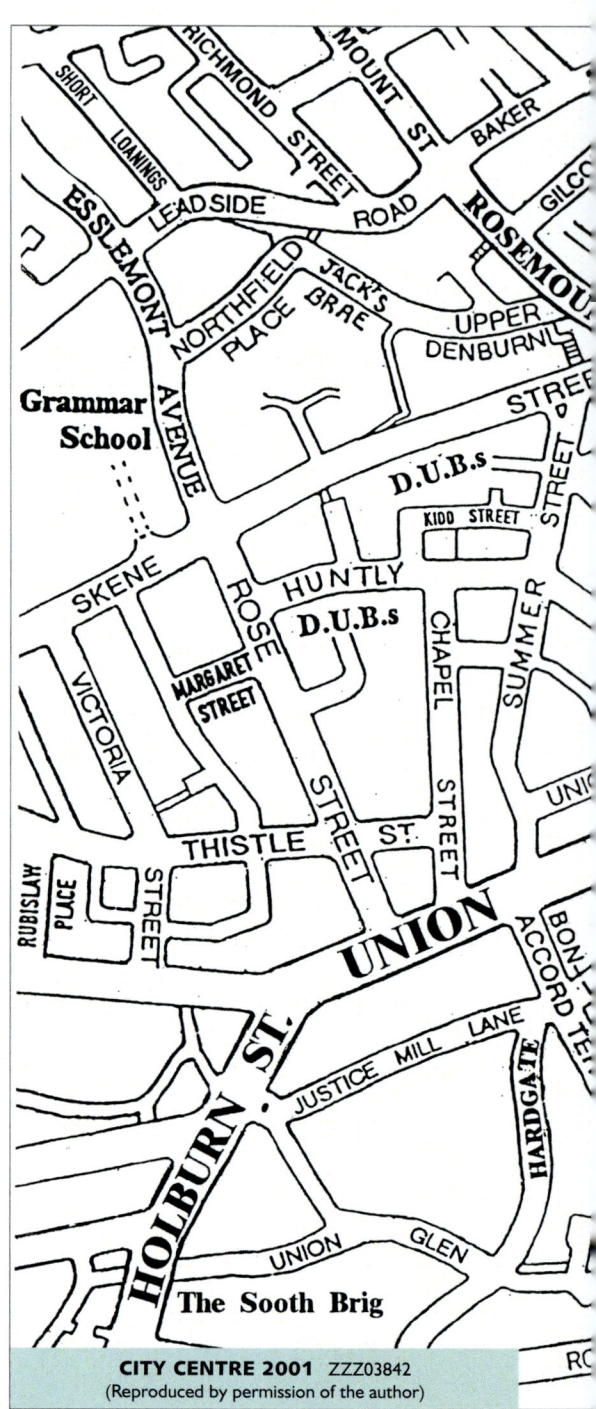

CITY CENTRE 2001 ZZZ03842
(Reproduced by permission of the author)

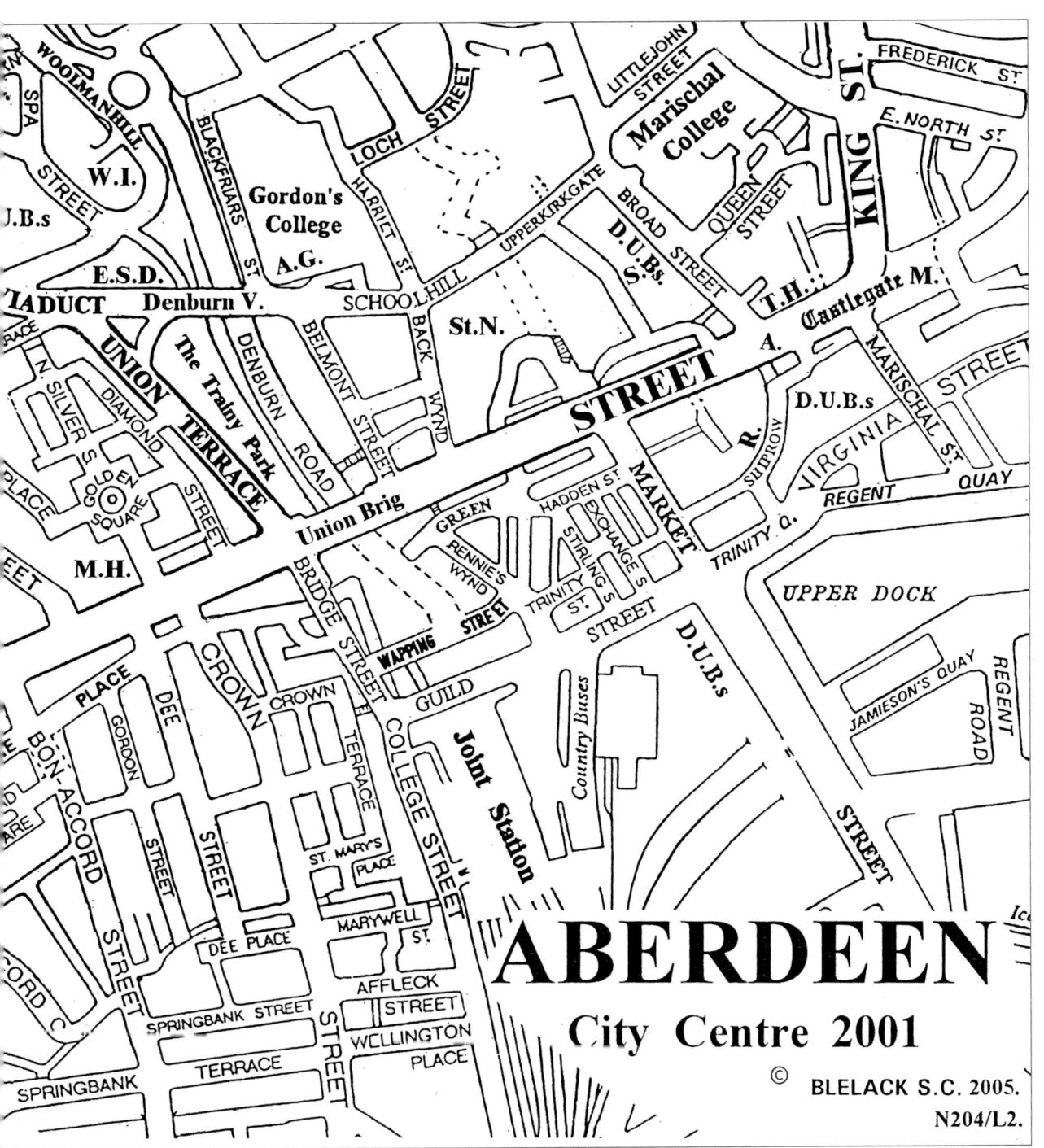

The viaduct streets still dominate the centre. AG is the Art Gallery. ESD is Education, Salvation and Damnation. MH is the Music Hall. WI is the old Royal Infirmary at Woolmanhill.

THE HARBOUR c1900 A90312

A century ago, steamships were dominant. Now it is oil industry supply vessels. Aberdeen is one of the few old-established harbours that are still full of commercial activity.

The council are keen to promote Aberdeen as a centre of new and ecologically sound energy production. There are even plans for a line of giant windmills just off the beach. This is a good direction to go, but it remains to be seen what comes of it all.

HIS MAJESTY'S THEATRE 1927 SA000033 (Detail)
(Courtesy of University of St Andrews Library)

A hundred years after construction, the theatre is being extended. This view from the east will not be seen again. The front of the extension is all glass modernity, but the tall east side, rising from the ground through three storeys before reaching the level of the viaduct, shown here, is clad in granite from Kemnay. The only reason that any local granite is available is that the quarry was reopened to supply stone for the Scottish Parliament building, surely the one positive thing about that whole saga.

Another traditional source of work that has all but been abandoned is tourism. The hotels and boarding houses are doing well out of the oil industry and no serious effort has been made to re-establish the city as a holiday destination. There is much to see and admire in Aberdeen and many visitors are really impressed by the triumphant individuality of the Granite City. But there is little to tell a visitor what there is to see.

Even if a tourist found his way to Old Aberdeen, a really beautiful, quiet and distinctive place, with a medieval cathedral and a medieval university in its midst, there are no easily discovered indications of what such a visitor might be seeing. But things may be changing. There is now a large, easily-read notice-board in the Castlegate explaining its history and the significance of some of the buildings, and another in the kirkyard, telling of some of the prominent citizens buried there. Some of the office blocks built for the oil companies have been designed to be converted into hotels if they are not required for their original purpose. Here again, we shall see!

THE HEADQUARTERS OF THE NORTHERN ASSURANCE COMPANY, UNION STREET 1938 3A000013 (Detail)
(Courtesy of University of St Andrews Library)

A sign of the times. This impressive building, constructed in 1889, was the headquarters of the Northern Assurance Company when the company had established itself, not just in the north-east, but also in London. The columned entrance was a favourite meeting place for young people before a night out, and was known as the Monkey Hoos. It is now a pub!

No part of Britain can return to the mass holiday trade that faded in the sixties when the cheap flights to Spain became available. But Aberdeen is a unique city, startlingly different because of its granite construction and its austere style. It is also the gateway to Royal Deeside, surely at least the equal of the most beautiful place in the British Isles.

For those with a real interest in ancient history, we have the unique recumbent stone circles and the most concentrated selection of preserved castles in Britain.

PERSLEY DEN c1900 A90313

One of the most attractive features of Aberdeen is the fact that really beautiful and peaceful places are so readily accessible. Persley Den is just north of the Don and now within the city boundary, and walking here one could be in the middle of the countryside. The watercourse is not natural. It is part of the lade to Grandholm Mill and shows the extraordinary work done to bring water-power to the early mills.

The Scottish Parliament

The new Scottish Parliament met in the General Assembly Building, the Kirk's national headquarters. The Kirk requires its own building for one week each year, when the General Assembly meets. During this period in 2002, Parliament moved to Aberdeen, where it met from 28–30 May in the old library at King's College, which had been converted into a conference centre for the university's quincentenary in 1995. The old Scottish Parliament had met in various places before settling permanently in Edinburgh, but this was the first time that Parliament had met in Aberdeen. We are used to visits from the monarch. But when she came to Parliament, the MSPs of republican views held a somewhat childish boycott of the event.

KING JAMES IV'S ARMS 2005 ZZZ03840 (Norman Miller)

In the quad at King's College, these were restored to their full colourful glory for the visit of King James IV's thirteen-times-great-granddaughter in May 2002.

The greatest asset for future development and prosperity that Aberdeen has is her tradition of higher education. The University of Aberdeen is making efforts, with some success, to be in the highest category of the universities of this country. This is especially true in the fields of medicine and what is now called life sciences. (Academics cannot bring themselves to say 'biology' nowadays!) Much of the advanced work in these areas of study does not catch the headlines, but it is an important part of our efforts as a nation to remain in the forefront of intellectual and economic development.

The first iron lung in Britain was produced in Aberdeen in 1933. Dr Robert Henderson, a senior doctor at the City Hospital, bought all the parts with his own money and worked with John Mitchell, the hospital's engineer. He was criticised by the Medical Officer of Health for doing unauthorised work! Dr Henderson was awarded the CBE in 1947 for his work on artificial respirators.

More recently, the magnetic resonance imaging (MRI) scanner was developed at the medical school by a team led by Dr John Mallard. These two achievements alone would provide an impressive case for claiming to be something special.

The university includes the first centre for the study of organic agriculture in Britain. HRH the Duke of Rothesay (known in other parts of Britain as the Prince of Wales) came to open it officially in 1998.

As well as the two universities there is a long tradition of specialist, innovative research here. The Marine Laboratory, which does research into aspects of the fishing industry, is expected in what was, until recently, Scotland's biggest fishing port. The MacAulay Land Use Institute (formerly, the MacAulay Institute for Soil Research) is another long-term contributor to the north-east's status as a leading area of intellectual effort.

But the most significant of all is the Rowett Research Institute. Dr John Boyd Orr, finding

UNION STREET 1938 SA000014 (Detail) (Courtesy of University of St Andrews Library)

The screen of granite columns by John Smith, 1829, was designed to mark the change from the commerce of the street to the sacred space of the kirkyard, as it still does. The extravagant memorial that can be seen behind the facade is that of Robert Hamilton, Professor of Mathematics, who died in the year of the facade's construction. He used his knowledge of his subject to demonstrate that the government's plan for paying off the national debt was unworkable.

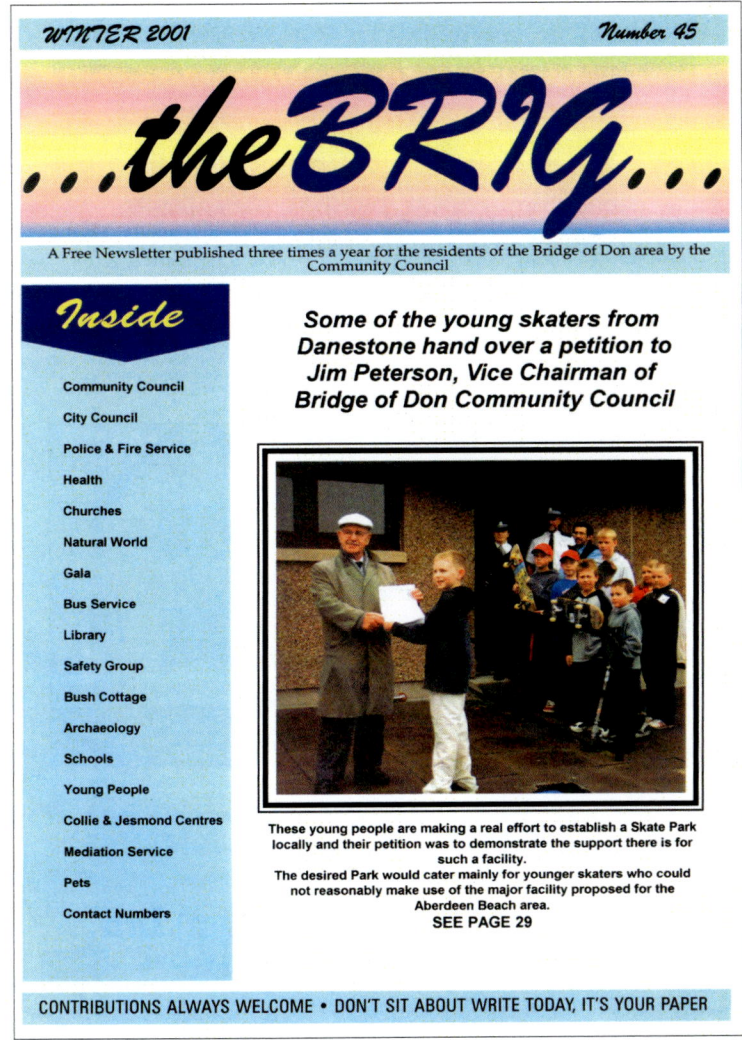

THE BRIG 2001 ZZZ03853
(Reproduced by kind permission of the editor)

Bridge of Don is has a large population, but no centre to give the sort of focus that many old but smaller places have. However, it does have a very active community council, which negotiates on its behalf with the city authorities. It also produces 'The Brig', which is distributed to every house in the area free, thrice a year.

and Agriculture Organisation. He was awarded the Nobel Peace Prize in 1949 and later ennobled by the British government.

A few years into the 21st century, and despite all the efforts of the town planners, Aberdeen remains the Granite City. This is true of much of the city centre, Rosemount, the West End, Ferryhill, Torry and some other areas. It is largely true of Old Aberdeen, although here freestone is also to be seen.

The threat of Aberdeen's reduction to a faceless provincial town, like any other in the world, still exists. The mindless modernisers and the architects and developers will continue to try to bring this to pass. More will be lost. But the pace of demolition has slowed from the days of the Comprehensive Central Destruction Area.

himself the director of a research institute that did not really exist, set about raising the finance himself. He was extremely successful. Rowett Research, named after its major contributor, opened in 1922. Working first on animal nutrition, the work was extended to human nutrition in the 1930s. The Institute gained a world-wide reputation, as did Dr Boyd Orr, sixty-five years old in 1945, who was appointed head of the United Nations Food

TENEMENT ROOFSCAPE 2005 A90727k (Norman Miller)

Restrained embellishment of the top makes interesting viewing for those who bother to look. This one is in Victoria Road, Torry.

Aberdeen is, essentially, a very pleasant place to live. It is clean and reasonably green, small enough not to be crushingly anonymous, as big cities easily can be, and yet large enough to have the cultural facilities that only a city can provide. Many come as students from quite different places and find that they actually would like to continue to live and work here.

Many of the exceptionally severe neo-classical buildings of the late 18th and early 19th centuries are still standing. They, and the later more elaborate granite buildings, complement each other to create the distinctive presence of the city, so dramatic and unmistakable, and so much in tune with the geographical and social context in which the city exists. There is a history of remarkable achievement by a few talented individuals and, more importantly, a tradition of achievement by ordinary folk working to make a success of their lives, often against the odds. We have not won Britain in Bloom for some years, but Hazlehead was officially Britain's Best Public Park 2004.

The city's official greeting to departing guests is:

'Happy to meet. Sorry to part.
Happy to meet again.
Bon-Accord.'

Some Hope for the Future

Even if the authorities do not care and do not understand the importance of preserving the unique history of the city, there are others who do. Three local heritage societies exist, as well as branches of several national bodies. It is significant that the local societies are to be found in the ancient and academic Old Aberdeen, the genteel and residential Ferryhill and the industrial and proletarian Torry.

SATROSPHERE 2005 A90710k (Norman Miller)

In a new use for beautiful old buildings, this is the city's science museum. The building on the right was the depot for the beach trams.

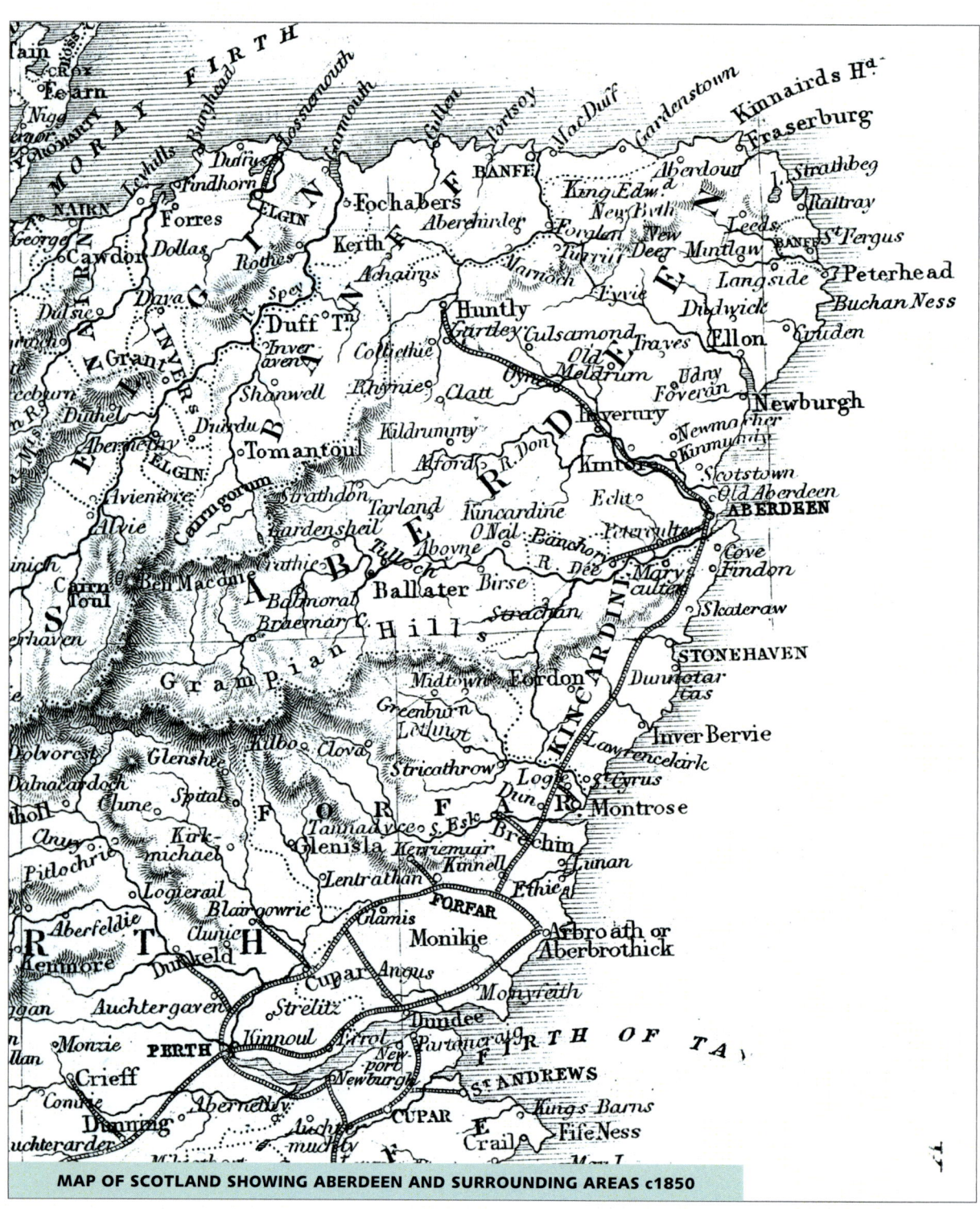

MAP OF SCOTLAND SHOWING ABERDEEN AND SURROUNDING AREAS c1850

ACKNOWLEDGEMENTS:
I wish to acknowledge the support and encouragement of my fellow-members of the Old Aberdeen Heritage Society. I am most grateful for the forbearance of my sister, Mrs Isobel Hunter, without whose frequent assistance with the camera and computer, I would have been unable to start this project.

Photographs used by courtesy of University of St Andrews Library are reproduced from digital copies held in the University of St Andrews Library. For further information about the collections, obtaining copies of images, or authorisation to reproduce them, please refer to http://specialcollections.st-and.ac.uk or contact Department of Special Collections, University of St Andrews Library, North Street, St Andrews, Fife KY16 9TR (tel 01334-462339; email speccoll@st-and.ac.uk)

BIBLIOGRAPHY:

A Thousand Years of Aberdeen — Alexander Keith, Aberdeen University Press

City by the Gray North Sea — Fenton Wyness, Impulse Books.

Aberdeen: An Illustrated Architectural Guide — W A Brogden, The Rutland Press

The Admirable Mechanic — Moira Henderson, Aberdeen City Libraries.

Aberdeen Before 1800 — Edited by E Patricia Dennison, David Ditchburn and Michael Lynch, Tuckwell Press

Aberdeen 1800 – 2000 — Edited by A Hamish Fraser and Clive H Lee, Tuckwell Press

The Villages of Aberdeen (series): Old Aberdeen, Spital, The Spital Lands and Others — Diane Morgan, Denburn Books.

Maritime Aberdeen — John Edwards, Tempus Publishing

The Granite City and The Hidden City — Robert Smith, John Donald Publishers

The Aberdeen Granite Industry — Tom Donnelly, University of Aberdeen Centre for Scottish Studies

Grit, Growth and Sometimes Groovy: Aberdeen in the Sixties — Griselda Sarah McGregor, Keith Murray Publications

Aberdeen Curiosities — Robert Smith, John Donald Publishers

Aberdeen in the General Strike — Liz Kibblewhite and Andy Rigby, Aberdeen People's Press

Images of Aberdeen — Raymond Anderson, Breedon Books

Frae a' the Airts to Haudigain — Fullerton Court and Murray Court Oral History Group, Aberdeen City Council

Work, Welfare and the Price of Fish — David Atherton (project leader), Aberdeen City Council

The City and its Worlds — Terry Brotherston and Donald J Wirthrington, Cruithne Press

Aberdeen in the Nineteenth Century — John S Smith and David Stevenson, Aberdeen University Press

Scottish Samurai Thomas Blake Glover — Alexander McKay, Canongate Books

Indian Peter — Douglas Skelton, Mainstream Publishing

Blood and Granite: True Crime in Aberdeen — Norman Adams, Black and White Publishing.

Aberdeens of the World — Frederick Bull, Scottish Cultural Press.

Francis Frith
Pioneer Victorian Photographer

Francis Frith, founder of the world-famous photographic archive, was a multi-talented man. A devout Quaker and a highly successful Victorian businessman, he was philosophical by nature and pioneering in outlook. By 1855 he had already established a wholesale grocery business in Liverpool, and sold it for the astonishing sum of £200,000, which is the equivalent today of over £15,000,000. Now in his thirties, and captivated by the new science of photography, Frith set out on a series of pioneering journeys up the Nile and to the Near East.

He was the first photographer to venture beyond the sixth cataract of the Nile. Africa was still the mysterious 'Dark Continent', and Stanley and Livingstone's historic meeting was a decade into the future. The conditions for picture taking confound belief. He laboured for hours in his wicker dark-room in the sweltering heat of the desert, while the volatile chemicals fizzed dangerously in their trays. Back in London he exhibited his photographs and was 'rapturously cheered' by members of the Royal Society. His reputation as a photographer was made overnight.

By the 1870s the railways had threaded their way across the country, and Bank Holidays and half-day Saturdays had been made obligatory by Act of Parliament. All of a sudden the working man and his family were able to enjoy days out, take holidays, and see a little more of the world.

With typical business acumen, Francis Frith foresaw that these new tourists would enjoy having souvenirs to commemorate their days out. For the next thirty years he travelled the country by train and by pony and trap, producing fine photographs of seaside resorts and beauty spots that were keenly bought by millions of Victorians. These prints were painstakingly pasted into family albums and pored over during the dark nights of winter, rekindling precious memories of summer excursions. Frith's studio was soon supplying retail shops all over the country, and by 1890 F Frith & Co had become the greatest specialist photographic publishing company in the world, with over 2,000 sales outlets, and pioneered the picture postcard.

Francis Frith had died in 1898 at his villa in Cannes, his great project still growing. By 1970 the archive he created contained over a third of a million pictures showing 7,000 British towns and villages.

Frith's legacy to us today is of immense significance and value, for the magnificent archive of evocative photographs he created provides a unique record of change in the cities, towns and villages throughout Britain over a century and more. Frith and his fellow studio photographers revisited locations many times down the years to update their views, compiling for us an enthralling and colourful pageant of British life and character.

We are fortunate that Frith was dedicated to recording the minutiae of everyday life. For it is this sheer wealth of visual data, the painstaking chronicle of changes in dress, transport, street layouts, buildings, housing and landscape that captivates us so much today, offering us a powerful link with the past and with the lives of our ancestors.

Computers have now made it possible for Frith's many thousands of images to be accessed almost instantly. The archive offers every one of us an opportunity to examine the places where we and our families have lived and worked down the years. Its images, depicting our shared past, are now bringing pleasure and enlightenment to millions around the world a century and more after his death. For further information visit: **www.francisfrith.com**

FRITH PRODUCTS & SERVICES

Francis Frith would doubtless be pleased to know that the pioneering publishing venture he started in 1860 still continues today. Over a hundred and forty years later, The Francis Frith Collection continues in the same innovative tradition and is now one of the foremost publishers of vintage photographs in the world. Some of the current activities include:

INTERIOR DECORATION

Today Frith's photographs can be seen framed and as giant wall murals in thousands of pubs, restaurants, hotels, banks, retail stores and other public buildings throughout the country. In every case they enhance the unique local atmosphere of the places they depict and provide reminders of gentler days in an increasingly busy and frenetic world.

PRODUCT PROMOTIONS

Frith products are used by many major companies to promote the sales of their own products or to reinforce their own history and heritage. Frith promotions have been used by Hovis bread, Courage beers, Scots Porage Oats, Colman's mustard, Cadbury's foods, Mellow Birds coffee, Dunhill pipe tobacco, Guinness, and Bulmer's Cider.

GENEALOGY AND FAMILY HISTORY

As the interest in family history and roots grows world-wide, more and more people are turning to Frith's photographs of Great Britain for images of the towns, villages and streets where their ancestors lived; and, of course, photographs of the churches and chapels where their ancestors were christened, married and buried are an essential part of every genealogy tree and family album.

FRITH PRODUCTS

All Frith photographs are available Framed or just as Mounted Prints and unmounted versions. These may be ordered from the address below. Other products available are - Calendars, Jigsaws, Canvas Prints, Mugs, Tea Towels, Tableware and local and prestige books.

THE INTERNET

Over several hundred thousand Frith photographs can be viewed and purchased on the internet through the Frith websites!

For more detailed information on Frith products, look at
www.francisfrith.com

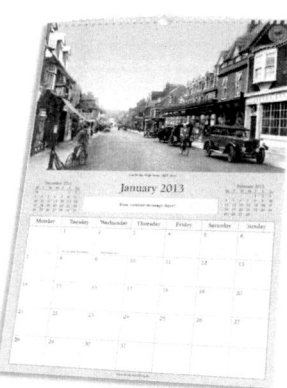

See the complete list of Frith Books at: www.francisfrith.com
This web site is regularly updated with the latest list of publications from The Francis Frith Collection. If you wish to buy books relating to another part of the country that your local bookshop does not stock, you may purchase on-line.

For further information, trade, or author enquiries please contact us at the address below:
The Francis Frith Collection, Unit 19 Kingsmead Business Park, Gillingham, Dorset SP8 5FB.
Tel: +44 (0)1722 716 376   Email: sales@francisfrith.co.uk

See Frith products on the internet at www.francisfrith.com

FREE PRINT OF YOUR CHOICE
CHOOSE A PHOTOGRAPH FROM THIS BOOK
+ POSTAGE

Mounted Print
Overall size 14 x 11 inches (355 x 280mm)

TO RECEIVE YOUR FREE PRINT

Choose any Frith photograph in this book

Simply complete the Voucher opposite and return it with your payment (to cover postage and handling) and we will print the photograph of your choice in SEPIA (size 11 x 8 inches) and supply it in a cream mount ready to frame (overall size 14 x 11 inches).

Order additional Mounted Prints
at HALF PRICE - £19.00 each (normally £38.00)

If you would like to order more Frith prints from this book, possibly as gifts for friends and family, you can buy them at half price (with no additional postage costs).

Have your Mounted Prints framed

For an extra £20.00 per print you can have your mounted print(s) framed in an elegant polished wood and gilt moulding, overall size 16 x 13 inches (no additional postage required).

IMPORTANT!

❶ Please note: aerial photographs and photographs with a reference number starting with a "Z" are not Frith photographs and cannot be supplied under this offer.

❷ Offer valid for delivery to one UK address only.

❸ These special prices are only available if you use this form to order. You must use the ORIGINAL VOUCHER on this page (no copies permitted). We can only despatch to one UK address.

❹ This offer cannot be combined with any other offer.

As a customer your name & address will be stored by Frith but not sold or rented to third parties. Your data will be used for the purpose of this promotion only.

Send completed Voucher form to:
The Francis Frith Collection,
1 Chilmark Estate House, Chilmark,
Salisbury, Wiltshire SP3 5DU

Voucher for **FREE** and Reduced Price Frith Prints

Please do not photocopy this voucher. Only the original is valid, so please fill it in, cut it out and return it to us with your order.

Picture ref no	Page no	Qty	Mounted @ £19.00	Framed + £20.00	Total Cost £
		1	Free of charge*	£	£
			£19.00	£	£
			£19.00	£	£
			£19.00	£	£
			£19.00	£	£
			£19.00	£	£

Please allow 28 days for delivery. Offer available to one UK address only

* Post & handling	£3.80
Total Order Cost	£

Title of this book . . . .

I enclose a cheque/postal order for £ . . . .
made payable to 'Heritage Resource Management Ltd'

OR please debit my Mastercard / Visa / Maestro card, details below

Card Number:

Issue No (Maestro only):   Valid from (Maestro):

Card Security Number: Expires:

Signature:

Name Mr/Mrs/Ms . . . .

Address . . . .

. . . .

. . . .

. . . . Postcode . . . .

Daytime Tel No . . . .

Email . . . .

Valid to 31/12/26

Free Print – see overleaf

Can you help us with information about any of the Frith photographs in this book?

We are gradually compiling an historical record for each of the photographs in the Frith archive. It is always fascinating to find out the names of the people shown in the pictures, as well as insights into the shops, buildings and other features depicted.

If you recognize anyone in the photographs in this book, or if you have information not already included in the author's caption, do let us know. We would love to hear from you, and will try to publish it in future books or articles.

An Invitation from The Francis Frith Collection to Share Your Memories

The 'Share Your Memories' feature of our website allows members of the public to add personal memories relating to the places featured in our photographs, or comment on others already added. Seeing a place from your past can rekindle forgotten or long held memories. Why not visit the website, find photographs of places you know well and add YOUR story for others to read and enjoy? We would love to hear from you!

www.francisfrith.com/memories

Our production team

Frith books are produced by a small dedicated team at offices near Salisbury. Most have worked with the Frith Collection for many years. All have in common one quality: they have a passion for the Frith Collection.

Frith Books and Gifts

We have a wide range of books and gifts available on our website utilising our photographic archive, many of which can be individually personalised.

www.francisfrith.com